W9-CLK-743

A Short History of Guatemala

by

Ralph Lee Woodward, Jr.
Emeritus Professor of History,
Tulane University

Editorial Laura Lee
Guatemala, 2005

ISBN 99922-797-2-9

Editorial Laura Lee
Apartado Postal #384
La Antigua, Guatemala, C. A.
lauralee@conexion.com

Cover design and layout
Guisela Asensio Lueg

Other books on Guatemala in English
by Ralph Lee Woodward, Jr.:

Class Privilege and Economic Development: The Consulado de Comercio of Guatemala, 1793–1871 (University of North Carolina Press, 1966)

Guatemala (Clio Press, 1992)

Rafael Carrera and the Emergence of the Republic of Guatemala, 1821–1871 (University of Georgia Press, 1993)

For Nichole, Michael, and Isabelle

Table of Contents

GUATEMALA
MEXICO
BELIZE
HONDURAS
EL SALVADOR
PACIFIC OCEAN
Gulf of Honduras
Guatemala
Belmopan
San Salvador
Flores
Cobán
Huehuetenango
Quetzaltenango
Escuintla
Puerto Barrios
National capital
Departmental capital
Town, village
Major airport
Volcano
Archaeological site
International boundary
Departmental boundary
Pan American Highway
Main road
Railroad
The boundaries and names shown and the designations used on this map do not imply official endorsement or acceptance by the United Nations.
Where the names of the departments are the same as their capitals, only the capitals are named.
Map No. 3834 Rev. 3 UNITED NATIONS
May 2004
Department of Peacekeeping Operations
Cartographic Section

1

The Land of the Maya

Tikal

The enchanting Central American country of Guatemala is at the same time both unique and remarkably representative of Latin America. There is certainly no other country quite like it, and yet it has so many of the characteristics often described as "Latin American" that it has been a laboratory for academic studies by historians, anthropologists, political scientists, and other scholars. It is a land that reflects well the mixing of native American and European peoples from the sixteenth century, with a smaller African element also present. It is a land with breathtaking geographical beauty as well as violent earthquakes and volcanoes so that its natural history imposes a dramatic and powerful influence on its human history. It is a land where military force over the centuries has played an inordinately important role in its political development. It is a land that came to depend on single agricultural commodities—cacao, cochineal, coffee, bananas—for its economic development. It is a land whose administration has often been marked by corruption, graft, and irresponsibility. And it is a land where personal influence and contacts play more than a minor role in getting things done and where extraordinary individuals have often played a major role in changing the course of its history. These are all characteristics often attributed to Latin America in general, yet unlike Guatemala, few countries have them all.

The Guatemalan highlands are blessed with natural beauty, fertile valleys, and a delightful climate, but more than anything else, Guatemala's large and colorful indigenous population is what sets it apart from other countries in the Western Hemisphere. The present-day area of Guatemala was at the heart of one of the three great pre-Columbian civilizations. In South America the Inca Empire stretched from Colombia to the Argentine, while in the North the Nahuatl, or Aztec, civilization covered much of modern-day Mexico, but it was in Central America where the earliest of these advanced civilizations—the Maya—thrived for centuries. Earlier indigenous civilizations prepared the way for all of these civilizations. In the case of the Maya, the Olmec people that developed in the coastal region around Veracruz during the first millennium B.C. preceded later Maya development to the South. As early as 2500 B.C. there were productive villages in Guatemala that traded foodstuffs and pottery. The Maya developed slowly and would not reach the peak of its classical civilization until 600–900 A.D. Unlike the Inca or Aztec nations, however, the Maya did not evolve into a unified state, instead developing clusters of communities into many city-states. What unity existed among them was cultural rather than political.

In the Guatemalan highlands thriving communities emerged during the first millennium B.C. in many separate nations or cultural units. As many as thirty different linguistic dialects differentiated these peoples. Relations among these separate nations were not always peaceful. They influenced each other through trade or conquest, and exerted substantial cultural influence on their neighbors. Their markets reflected trade from great distances and well worn paths created a network of commerce throughout the highlands. By 500 B.C. an advanced civilization with a rising population flourished in highland Guatemala. The archeological site of Kaminaljuyú, in the outskirts of modern Guatemala City, reveals an ancient city populated by thousands. By the beginning of the Christian era, a thriving Maya civilization reflected considerable influence from Olmec culture in Mexico, while its own influence extended southward at least as far as Nicaragua and Costa Rica.

Perhaps because of overpopulation in the highlands, combined with natural disasters such as earthquakes or volcanic eruptions, there was significant migration from the highlands into the lowland Petén region of northern Guatemala. It was here that the Maya reached their highest cultural achievements in what has become known as the Classic Maya period (250–900 A.D.), although there is increasing evidence that some Maya centers, including El Mirador and Cival, had already reached a high level of civilization even before that time. Maya scientists made advances in astronomy and mathematics comparable to those of ancient Egypt. They evolved a complex written language with hieroglyphs recorded on stelae—stone monuments erected at regular intervals throughout Maya territory—that reflected major historical figures and events. Only recently deciphered, archaeologists are now able to reconstruct much more detail on these people than was known formerly. Great cities arose around ceremonial religious centers in a cluster of sites in the northern Petén—Tikal, Uaxactún, El Mirador, and Yaxha—with many others elsewhere in northern Guatemala and in what is today Chiapas and Honduras. Quiriguá is a notable Classic Maya site located just off the main highway from Guatemala City to the Caribbean ports.

Maya artistic and scientific achievements were phenomenal. They developed an accurate calendar and complex organizational skills. Their art work survives in painted pottery, stone carving, and in a few ancient textiles. Their architectural monuments were remarkable, if not the equal of ancient Greek and Roman or medieval European builders. They did not, however, develop energy-saving machines, nor did they exploit the wheel, even though their children played with wheeled toys. Lacking domesticated animals, they depended entirely on the labor of humans working directly with their hands under the supervision of a small elite class.

About 900 A.D. the Maya migrated northward once again, deeper into what is today Mexico. During this Post-Classic period, (900–1200 A.D.) new cities emerged in the Usumacinta Valley and in the Chiapas lowlands, notably at Palenque, Piedras Negras, Bonampak, Yaxchilán, and Altar de Sacrificios and in the Yucatán peninsula at Dzibilchaltún, Uxmal, Kabah, Sayhil, and elsewhere. These cities also had impressive architectural monuments—great stone pyramids that still stand—although surrounded by the jungle. In the Late Post-Classic period (c.1200–1530) Mexican Toltecs invaded Yucatán and made Chichén Itzá their capital. Scientific and artistic achievements were less remarkable than earlier advances in the Petén cities and at Quiriguá and at Copán in Honduras. Yet the relative absence of technological improvement kept their economies underdeveloped. As the population grew, warfare among city states became more common. Internal civil warfare and intervention from central Mexican peoples sapped Maya strength and vitality. By the time of the Spanish Conquest, the Maya and their lowland civilization were in serious decline, yet they resisted subjugation longer than either the Aztecs of Mexico or the Inca of Peru.

Meanwhile, Mayas retreating from the Spaniards back into the Petén from Yucatán founded a new city, Tayasal, near Tikal. Tayasal produced no great archaeological monuments, but was a place of refuge during a time of decline. It maintained Maya autonomy in the region until 1697. Elsewhere, the Lacandón, descendants of the people who had built the magnificent temples at Palenque and Bonampak, found security in remote jungle and mountain villages, and they defied pacification throughout the Hispanic period and raided Spanish-controlled areas from time to time. Spanish counter-offensives from both Guatemala and Yucatán repeatedly failed.

While the magnificent ceremonial sites of the lowland Maya—with their temples, pyramids, ball courts, and evidence of advanced civilization—are highly impressive, of perhaps greater significance for modern Guatemala were those who stayed behind, those who remained in the highlands and maintained a viable agricultural society around small communities. Several separate nations developed there. They, too, had cities and ceremonial centers and continued to support large populations. Noteworthy archaeological ruins remain of those cities at Zaculeu, in Huehuetenango, capital of the Mam Maya; at Iximché, near Tecpán, capital of the Kaqchikel; at Utatlán, near Santa Cruz del Quiché, capital of the K'iche'; and at Mixco Viejo on the Río Motagua, capital of the Pocomam. By the end of the fourteenth century, three of these nations had become dominant. The strongest was the K'iche', controlling much of the western highlands around modern-day Quetzaltenango. To the east were the Kaqchikel, and between the two, around Lake Atitlán were the Tz'utujil. These peoples all developed strong agricultural societies centered around production of corn, but they also grew many other fruits and vegetables and produced notable weaving and pottery that they traded widely in native markets.

The principal occupation of nearly all pre-Columbian Guatemalans was agriculture—the growing of corn (maize), tubers, beans, fruits, vegetables, and cotton. The ruined Maya cities reflect for the most part ceremonial, religious, or governmental activities, which had relatively little to do with the daily life of the peasants who worked the soil and lived on the outskirts of these centers. The daily routine remains the same in many indigenous communities even today. Most lived in straw or palm-covered houses with walls made of adobe, wooden poles, or even cornstalks, depending on the climate and region. Only the important people in the great cities lived in houses of stone.

Survival has been a powerful characteristic of Guatemala's indigenous peoples since before the Conquest. They maintained their community life with remarkable consistency over the past five centuries. A pattern of life not unlike that of pre-conquest times is still evident in rural, highland Guatemala, where a few "rich" families own much of the land and animals. Although they are wealthy by village standards and occupy important posts in the village social and religious life, they continue to work with their hands—their counterparts in the European society do not. A sort of middle class own some land, a few animals, and are assured generally of a modest but regular income. The poor, who are in the great majority, have tiny plots of land to farm and generally enough to eat, but they live a day-to-day existence. Many depend on charity and assistance from the community. The diet of nearly all the people remains much as it was before the Conquest. The Spaniards brought wheat, rice, and assorted fruits and vegetables, as well as livestock and poultry, and some of these commodities found their way into the indigenous diet, but not nearly so regularly as Indian maize, beans, and native fruits appeared on the conquerors' tables. Chocolate, for example, was a drink quickly picked up by the Spanish soldiers, even though their priests condemned it and associated it with heresy and sexual promiscuity.

In the highland indigenous communities the men tended the corn and other crops. The women ran their households and manufactured utensils, clothing, and housewares. A high degree of specialization evolved, as each village developed a particular craft or skill. Some engaged in cotton spinning and weaving, or pottery-making. Others manufactured jewelry, basketry, musical instruments, toys, tools, or furniture. Merchants carried these objects far and wide to the village marketplaces, a practice that still continues in Guatemala. They raised and traded indigo, cochineal, and a wide assortment of dyewoods to give their clothing and bodies bright colors. Financing of this activity was primitive. Barter was common, but semiprecious stones and cacao beans served as a kind of currency until the Spanish introduced metal coins in the sixteenth century. Metalwork was not among the highland Maya skills, although they did acquire some metal goods from other Indians to the north or south.

The cornfields, or *milpas*, were and are the key to life in the indigenous villages, and around their use revolved the social and economic status of the individual. Private ownership was not a highly developed concept in pre-Columbian society, although it seems to have been evolving by the time of the Spanish Conquest. Communally-owned land was the norm, and such land ownership persisted into modern times. But Spanish emphasis on privately-owned land challenged and altered indigenous landholding patterns.

For most of the Maya, education consisted of learning the vocations and practices of their parents. Only the children of the priests and the ruling families received formal education. They learned reading, writing, and natural and social sciences, including the arts of war and government. In fact, their educational system was not unlike that of Europe of the same period, where only the privileged received education, and that closely supervised by religious authorities.

The Maya observed strict moral codes regarding sexual behavior. Generally, each man had but one wife, although there were exceptions, notably among the Lacandón, where polygamy was common. Also, the chiefs and nobles often kept concubines. There were prostitutes, and they were recognized, but their social status was low. Fathers arranged marriages, but the children usually participated in the selection process. Marriages could be terminated relatively easily, and the child of a dissolved union accompanied the parent of his or her own sex. Harsh penalties proscribed fornication and other sexual offenses. An outraged husband had the right to smash the head of an adulterer with a large rock. Rape was also punishable by death. Other rules prohibited or restricted sexual relations with and among slaves. Homosexuality also existed among the Maya, but not a great deal is known as to the extent of its acceptance.

Agricultural societies are seldom noted for their development of recreation or the arts, yet the Maya excelled here. They played various kinds of ball games, although the formal ball courts of Maya ruins were primarily ritualistic or ceremonial centers, not amusement fields. They played several wind and percussion instruments, but not the marimba, so popular in modern Guatemala, which undoubtedly had African origins. Maya art reflected assorted athletic contests as well as a lifestyle closely connected with religious beliefs. Painting must have been a popular art, for murals ornamented the great halls of the cities. The Maya also painted their pottery, both fine and crude, as well as the walls of private homes and even peasant huts. Religious and mythological motifs characterized much of this painting.

Religion permeated Maya life. The priests were the most powerful members of Maya society. Government was theocratic, almost completely so, as priests not only directed the religious and cultural development, but advised and dictated to the civil rulers as well. A philosophy of good versus evil, with appropriate deities representing elements and characteristics, was at the heart of the religion. The practice of human sacrifice was never really characteristic of the highland Maya. The Aztec had introduced this practice in Maya territory in Yucatán by the time the Spanish arrived, and the horrified conquistadors wrote luridly about it there. In some areas, Christian teachings combined with the native religions, so that crucifixion became an added means of human sacrifice.

While the priests developed a complex theology, most of the people clung to a simpler religion and a concept of good versus evil in which omens, symbols, and superstitions were important. Much of this symbolism, mixed with Christian symbolism and mythology after the Conquest, survives in the mountains of Guatemala and Chiapas. Maya accounts of the origin of man and the universe, recorded after the Conquest, were similar to the Judeo-Christian mythology and were doubtless influenced by it. With the destruction of the Maya temples and formal religion, Spanish priests encouraged and then required the Indians to adopt Christianity. Conversion was often incomplete, for Spanish Catholicism and the Maya religion had much in common. Both recognized and emphasized an eternal conflict between good and evil. The multitude of saints was not incongruous with the multitude of nature gods and symbolic gods of the Maya. Conveniently for the Europeans, the cross had been the symbol of the vital Maya rain god in some areas. Both religions gave priests a dominant role, with a close relation to political authority. Both peoples believed in life after death, yet both feared death, and both religions contained elaborate rituals for death and burial. The Maya practiced cremation, although not universally. In essence, the teachings of the Spanish friars were not wholly alien or strange to the Maya, and with the demise of their own religious leaders, the natives accepted the Spanish clerics relatively easily—considerably more easily than they accepted the Spanish soldiers! Thus the Church came to play a vital role in the pacification of the Maya. Religious organizations became intertwined with village government and society. At the local level, fraternal organizations, called *cofradías*, are still the most important social organizations in indigenous communities. Even so, the folk religion of today often bears only slight resemblance to Catholicism as it practiced in Europe, the United States, or non-Indian parts of Latin America.

Highland Maya history is steeped in the mythology that was passed on from generation to generation of Mayas, but not recorded in writing until after the arrival of the Spaniards. These include, most notably, the *Annals of the Cakchiquels* (1604) and the *Popol Vuh* (1704) in K'iche'. These works trace the ruling dynasties, but also reflect major events and views in their local history. Stone monuments, or *stelae*, at classic Mayan ruins, also recorded chronologies of dynasties in the lowland regions.

The indigenous religious traditions, with Christianity superimposed over them, together with the violence of the Conquest and the centuries of slavery or serfdom that followed, left clear impressions on the personality and mentality of the indigenous Guatemalan. To the outsider, including the Spaniard or creole in Guatemala, the Indian sometimes appears docile, obedient to authority, humble, and meek—as with lowered eyes and hat in hand he or she speaks respectfully to his landlord. Yet beneath this outward appearance lie deeper qualities and emotions of distrust and bitterness. The Maya worldview is oriented toward family and community, not toward the nation, which is alien to him or her. Patience, caution, stoicism, and reserve all characterize the modern Maya. Yet in their own villages they display humor, gaiety, and a wide range of emotions. They may appear dull to outsiders, when in fact they are quick to learn. They are often volatile and insistent, perfectly capable of demanding their rights. Indian rebellions, from the sixteenth through the twentieth centuries, testify to the indigenous love of liberty. Each village is a complete unit, with only secondary ties to other places and to the national structure. The indigenous residents of the village regard themselves as a "pueblo"—a sovereign people—proudly clinging to their traditional beliefs and values. Although these characteristics have helped the Indians of Guatemala to survive, they have also helped to maintain the cultural barriers that separate them from "modern" Guatemala. Indigenous isolation has never been absolute, however, and national policy and practice have inevitably impinged heavily on indigenous lifestyles and conditions.

The indigenous relation to the *ladinos*, as those of mixed European and Indian blood are called in Guatemala, and to the Europeans is often close and frequent, but there are significant differences between the ladinos and Indians. The Indians, the conquered, have learned to cushion the burden they carry for their white and ladino masters, and their personalities and lifestyles reflect centuries of oppression. The ladinos, on the other hand, have represented a growing middle sector—racially, culturally, economically, and socially—between the indigenous serfs and the privileged European upper class since the sixteenth century. Deprived of the deep traditional and ethnic roots of either the indigenous or the European, and denied easy acceptance by either, the ladinos have been more mobile and more aggressive, than either. They represent and typify most of Guatemala as it has developed since national independence. Even in communities where they are few in number, as in the western highlands, they are the more enterprising, the more aggressive, the more ambitious, and the more ruthless members of the community, seeking self-advancement by whatever means possible. They care less for abstract philosophical values, but are impressed by signs of material progress and by tangible means of joining in that progress. The ladinos are oriented toward the national life, toward the capital and sometimes beyond, while the indigenous people are oriented inwardly, toward their own immediate families and communities. Over the centuries these differences have become more cultural and economic than ethnic.

Population growth in the fifteenth century had placed extraordinary pressures on the highland Maya nations. Natural disasters and epidemic diseases added to their problems, which often led to war with neighboring peoples. Thus in 1501 the Kaqchikels defeated the Tz'utujil at Xacab. Although they failed to gain control of all of the Tz'utujil territory, they became a greater threat to the K'iche', especially when they allied with Mexicans (Aztecs) in 1512. Their war with the K'iche' dragged on for seven years, weakening both sides. Early in the struggle, as the Kaqchikel seemed to be gaining, a severe locust plague struck the Kaqchikel region, creating famine and checking their gains. Then, in 1514, a great fire destroyed their capital at Iximché.

Rumors of the arrival of the Spanish on the Caribbean coast led to a truce in 1519, and soon thereafter an epidemic of smallpox, unwittingly brought to the New World by the Spaniards, took a frightening toll on both sides, but especially among the already weakened Kaqchikel. Perhaps taking advantage of this weakened condition, the K'iche' resumed the war in 1521. The Kaqchikel, finding their Aztec allies now conquered, sent an emissary to the Spanish conquerors seeking aid. Pedro de Alvarado and a conquering army would bring that "aid" in 1524.

2

Europeanization

Pedro de Alvarado

The native peoples of Guatemala were familiar with catastrophe. They were fatalistic about their existence. Earthquakes, volcanoes, epidemics, climate changes, and warfare had all brought misery and dislocation to the Maya before the Spanish invasion of the sixteenth century. They had survived before and they would survive again, albeit not without massive alteration of the world as they knew it. The remarkable expansion of Renaissance Europe into the Americas that began with Christopher Columbus's voyage of 1492 did not take long to reach Guatemala. In 1502 Columbus, on his fourth voyage to America, sailed into the Gulf of Honduras and probably went ashore on Guatemala's north coast before continuing southeastward as far as Panama. Other Spanish explorers, Juan Díaz Solís and Vicente Yáñez, reached the same region in 1506.

Spanish conquistadors would soon thereafter occupy the isthmus from three different directions. The Spaniards had found scant precious metal in the Caribbean islands. They had quickly annihilated the primitive inhabitants, who failed to make good slaves. Early Spanish forays along the eastern coast of Central

America sought more slaves, but eventually led to conquest of the region. Álvaro Núñez de Balboa and then Pedro Arias de Ávila (Pedrarias Dávila) planted Spain's first American mainland colony in Panama. From there the Spanish advanced northward into Nicaragua and Honduras.

Other shipwrecked Spaniards had by 1511 already landed along the coast of Yucatán, where the natives, or Caribs who had fled from the islands to the mainland, quickly captured and sacrificed most of them to their gods or in some cases, we are told, cooked and ate them. These unfortunate Europeans had brought smallpox with them, however, which spread rapidly throughout the region, weakening resistance to later Spanish invaders. Yet one survivor, Gonzalo Guerrero, won the respect of local chiefs as he taught them how to resist the invaders. Perhaps coached by Guerrero, the Maya successfully defended Yucatán against an expedition by Francisco Hernández de Córdoba in 1517. Subsequent forays from Cuba against the Maya also failed but garnered some gold and turquoise jewelry that maintained the interest of the Cuban governor, Diego de Velásquez. Velásquez sent Fernando Cortez, who eventually defeated the Aztecs of Mexico in 1521, but in Yucatán he did little more than smash a few idols. Later, expeditions begun in 1527 under the leadership of Francisco de Montejo and his son finally overcame Maya resistance in Yucatán in 1546 after much bloodshed, but the final Spanish military victory over the lowland Maya did not come until 1697 at Tayasal, in the Petén region of northern Guatemala.

Once Cortez had crushed the Aztecs at Tenochtitlán (Mexico City), he ordered two expeditions into Central America, one overland and the other by sea. His naval commander, Cristóbal de Olid, sailed to the Gulf of Honduras and after formally establishing the town of Triunfo de la Cruz, declared himself independent of Cortez's authority, a practice common enough among the conquistador generation. Upon hearing of this, Cortez dispatched Francisco de las Casas with troops to relieve Olid, but soon thereafter decided to go himself. Marching overland across the jungles of the Petén in 1525, he succeeded in restoring his authority on the Honduran coast, but in the process seriously damaged his health. Before returning to Mexico in April 1526, Cortez consolidated his control of that region against the continuing efforts of Pedrarias Dávila to extend his authority into Honduras.

Meanwhile, Cortez's ambitious but loyal second-in-command, Pedro de Alvarado, left Mexico City in December 1523 in command of the overland expedition. His army included thousands of Tlaxcalans and other indigenous allies from central Mexico. Smallpox swept through the country ahead of him, making resistance light. From the isthmus of Tehuantepec the Spaniards had to fight their way into the rugged mountains of Chiapas and on into Guatemala, where the Kaqchikel and K'iche' peoples were warring. The smaller highland nations had allied to one or the other of these two powers. Following Cortez's example in Mexico, Alvarado took advantage of the enmities among the indigenous peoples. Allying with the Kaqchikel, together they defeated the K'iche' in April 1524. Alvarado himself reportedly met and killed the heroic K'iche' chief, Tecum-Umán, in hand-to-hand combat at Xelajú (near present-day Quetzaltenango, still known locally as "Xela").

Alvarado occupied the Kaqchikel capital at Iximché, near present-day Tecpán, renaming it "Guatemala," the Mexican Nahuatl name for the place. It commanded a high plateau, advantageous for defense, but in the face of a Kaqchikel rebellion, Alvarado soon found the location inconvenient and searched for a site with better access to water. In 1527 his brother, Jorge, thus established a new capital called Santiago de los Caballeros de Guatemala in the Almolonga Valley beneath Agua (Water) Volcano, so named for the lake in the crater atop this dormant volcano. Pedro de Alvarado spent two more years conquering the remainder of Guatemala and El Salvador and suppressing indigenous revolts. He laid out several new towns, but there were already many indigenous towns and villages that gradually became, to varying degrees, Hispanicized. Most of the Mexican (Tlaxcalan) troops that had accompanied Alvarado remained in Guatemala and settled in new towns and communities they established alongside the Maya people.

In Honduras, Alvarado faced the forces of Pedrarias Dávila of Nicaragua, and rivalry between these two conquerors led to dissension and disorder there for many years. Eventually, a series of royal decrees clarified the boundaries of the Kingdom of Guatemala in Alvarado's favor. It included what are today the republics of Costa Rica, Nicaragua, El Salvador, Honduras, and Guatemala, as well as Belize and the present Mexican state of Chiapas. After a triumphant visit to Spain in 1527, where he formally received the title of Governor and Captain General of Guatemala, Alvarado returned to the pacification of the isthmus. The scarcity of precious metals disappointed him, however, and when news arrived of Francisco Pizarro's discoveries in Peru, he headed for South America in 1534. Unwelcome there, he returned once more to Spain, where his wife, Francisca de la Cueva, had died in 1528. Alvarado now married her sister, Doña Beatriz de Alva de la Cueva. Accompanied by his new bride, he returned to Guatemala in 1539, but rumors of golden cities in Cíbola (North America) lured him north to Mexico. There he fought with his characteristic courage and recklessness in the Miztón War against the rebellious Chichimecas until he died in Guadalajara on 4 July 1541 after a horse fell upon him. Word of his death did not reach Santiago de Guatemala until 29 August, when a letter from the Viceroy of Mexico, Antonio de Mendoza, ordered Lieutenant Governor Francisco de la Cueva, a cousin of Alvarado's widow, to continue as governor in Guatemala. In her grief over the loss of her husband, Doña Beatriz reportedly wailed excessively, calling herself "*La sin ventura*" (the unfortunate or hapless one). Her tears were matched by unusually heavy rains that drenched

Guatemala in early September 1541. On 9 September the City Council and other notables including Alvarado's widow, met to install Lt. Governor de la Cueva as governor of the kingdom, but the strong-willed and ambitious Beatriz, supported by the powerful Bishop of Guatemala, Francisco Marroquín, managed to gain the support of most of those present and the council agreed to make her interim governor until the Spanish Crown decided the question. She was sworn in immediately along with her cousin Francisco, who continued as her Lt. Governor.

Beatriz would rule but a pair of days, however. The rains continued throughout Saturday, 10 September 1541, and on that night tremors from the nearby and active Fuego (Fire) Volcano caused the crater at the top of the Agua volcano to rupture. A torrent of water and mud gushed down the volcano's side carrying away part of the town and killing many people, including Doña Beatriz. Beatriz was one of only two women to serve as chief executive anywhere in Latin America throughout the Spanish colonial period, the other being Isabel de Bobadilla, the wife of Hernán de Soto, whom he left in charge of Cuba during his exploration of Florida (1539–1542), from which he never returned.

Francisco de la Cueva now succeeded to the governor's office provisionally. He and Bishop Marroquín supervised the construction of a new capital (present-day Antigua Guatemala) at the opposite end of the Almolonga Valley. De la Cueva then married Doña Leonor, the daughter of Pedro de Alvarado and Tlaxcalan Princess Doña Luisa de Xicotencatl, who had survived the destruction of the capital along with several ladies that Doña Beatriz had brought with her from Spain. These survivors were important in Guatemalan history as mothers of many of the principal families of the colonial era. Alvarado had no children by his de la Cueva wives. His legacy in Guatemala continued only through the descendants of his union with Doña Luisa.

As the conquest continued, settlers and adventurers from Spain, the Caribbean, and Mexico established towns throughout the isthmus, exploiting the native labor, and turning to agriculture when mining failed. Not all the indigenous people were servile, however, and revolts occurred throughout the colonial period and beyond. Alvarado himself crushed the first great revolt, that of the Kaqchikels, 1524–1530. Alvarado and other conquerors tried to maintain the servility of newly-conquered tribes by seizing chiefs (*caciques*) as hostages. The most notorious of these were the K'iche' and Kaqchikel chiefs, Sequechul and Sinacam, whom Alvarado held captive for sixteen years. Afraid that they were directing continued uprisings, even from captivity, Alvarado took them to Mexico with him in 1540, but after his death they escaped and were never heard from again. Indian rebellions and raids continued despite repeated expeditions against the fierce Lacandón of the Petén even as late as the eighteenth century. In the highlands, however, the Spanish succeeded in establishing their rule, although at the cost of thousands of Indian lives and heavy expenditures.

The Roman Catholic Church was an important partner in the Spanish Conquest of Guatemala, as priests accompanied the conquistadors and tried to establish Christianity among the natives as the soldiers brought them into subjugation. The efforts of Fray Bartolomé de las Casas, however, are a notable example of a peaceful approach by Christian friars to pacifying and exploiting the natives. Las Casas had seen the brutalities of the Conquest in Cuba and Hispaniola in the Caribbean. After his peaceful methods failed to pacify the Indians at Cumaná (in Venezuela), he cloistered himself for several years on the island of Hispaniola. Then he organized a Dominican convent at Granada, Nicaragua, where the cruel treatment of the Indians begun by Pedrarias had continued. Las Casas's preaching against such treatment was a thorn in the side of the settlers and civil officials there, but his efforts brought meager results. In 1536 he left Nicaragua for Guatemala. There he became a vocal conscience for Alvarado and the Spanish administrators. Reviving his idea of pacifying Indians unconquered by military force, in 1537 he began an experiment in the region north of the capital known as the Land of War because of the successful indigenous resistance to Spanish arms. Centering his activities at Tuzulutlán, he persuaded the caciques of the region to accept his friars, and his program prospered. That area became known as the Land of True Peace, or Verapaz. Las Casas returned to Spain, where his success in Guatemala aided him in persuading the Emperor Carlos V to issue, in 1542, the New Laws of the Indies, a serious attempt to stop the ruthless encomienda system.

Las Casas returned in 1544 as Bishop of Chiapas. There he continued his efforts with less success, for the outrage of the colonists against the New Laws made his work nearly impossible. Moreover, the Dominican experiment in the Verapaz eventually failed too, for Indians revolted and massacred friars. The Dominicans still maintained monasteries and lands in the Verapaz, but much of the province gradually fell under the control of settlers seeking land and labor. Nevertheless, the influence of Bartolomé de las Casas remained strong in Guatemala, and his call for humanity and compassion toward the indigenous peoples never disappeared altogether and continues today in the demands for human rights enforcement and social justice for the indigenous population.

The political structure of the Kingdom of Guatemala took shape slowly. Rivalry among the conquistadores led to disorder and turmoil, especially in Honduras and Nicaragua. Individual jealousies combined with geographical barriers worked against unity, so that virtually autonomous administrative centers emerged. In addition to Santiago de Guatemala, other major Spanish towns were Ciudad Real in Chiapas, Comayagua in Honduras, León and Granada in Nicaragua, and Panama City. Each new conquest justified a new government. The resulting decentralization undermined the efforts of royal agents to control the region. There was always a substantial gap between a theoretically highly centralized administrative empire and the actual decentralized system imposed by great distances and geographical barriers on the ground. Municipalities assumed authority and their town councils (*ayuntamientos*) were the most important governing bodies for they controlled jurisdiction over much wider areas than the towns themselves.

From Ralph Lee Woodward, Jr., *Central America: A Nation Divided*, 3rd ed., copyright © 1976, 1985, 1999 by Oxford University Press, Inc., p. 37. Used by permission of Oxford University Press, Inc.

By 1530 Guatemala, Nicaragua, Honduras, Chiapas, and Panama all functioned under separate royal orders. Yet in the following decade increased knowledge about the isthmus, the death of Pedrarias Dávila in Nicaragua, and the prestige of Pedro de Alvarado all contributed toward unification of the isthmus under a single jurisdiction. Establishment of the Viceroyalty of New Spain in 1535 implied Mexican rule over the northern portions of the region, but the establishment of the Audiencia de Panamá in the same year continued the confusion over jurisdiction in Nicaragua. Not until 1543 did the Crown politically unify Central America by creating the Audiencia de los Confines (Borders). This new court held jurisdiction from Tabasco and Yucatán to Panama, under the leadership of President Alonso de Maldonado, who was also the Governor of Guatemala. Searching for a centrally located capital, the Crown in 1544 ordered the new Audiencia to locate at Gracias, an early gold-mining boom town in the mountains of western Honduras. The residents of both Santiago de Guatemala and Panama City sent their agents (*procuradores*) to Spain to argue against Gracias. That town had flourished briefly from its mining importance, but the gold soon played out and the city was otherwise isolated and poorly located. In 1548, therefore, the Crown ordered the Audiencia moved to Santiago de Guatemala. Soon thereafter, the Audiencia lost jurisdiction over Panama, Yucatán, and Tabasco.

By this time there was nominal law and order, although indigenous revolts, new conquests, internal disputes, and attacks by foreign interlopers on both coasts would disrupt life on the isthmus periodically for more than two centuries thereafter. In the 1560s the Crown dissolved the Audiencia de los Confines and transferred its authority over Panama, Costa Rica, and Nicaragua to a new Audiencia at Panama. Guatemala, Honduras, and Chiapas now fell under the jurisdiction of the Audiencia of Mexico. But the indignant protests of powerful cacao producers and civil and ecclesiastical leaders—including Bartolomé de las

Casas, who believed that the Audiencia in Guatemala was a check against settlers' abuses of the Indian missions in Guatemala—brought a rapid reversal of this decision. By 1570 the Audiencia had been restored to Guatemala, with its jurisdiction stretching from Chiapas through Costa Rica. This jurisdiction survived beyond the end of Spanish rule. Meanwhile, King Felipe II granted the capital city the formal title of "Very Noble and Loyal City of Santiago de los Caballeros de Guatemala."

The province of Guatemala, which included present-day El Salvador, was easily the most important province in this Audiencia. The government in Guatemala paid less than adequate attention to the other provinces. Even within the province of Guatemala, the populous highland districts (Los Altos) around Quetzaltenango and the Pacific districts around San Salvador felt the discriminatory practices of the officials in the capital city. Santiago de Guatemala was not only the political, but also the social, economic, and ecclesiastical metropolis of the kingdom, and ambitious residents from all the provinces seeking to advance themselves gravitated there.

The Audiencia exercised executive, judicial, and legislative authority over the Kingdom. A president presided over this court of law, but the same individual was also the captain general with military authority and the governor with executive power, creating the tradition in Guatemala of a powerful chief executive. The Crown appointed the officers of the kingdom who usually served from four to seven years, except for the justices (*oidores*) of the Audiencia, who held their seats for life, or until they moved on to some other office. The tendency was for natives of Spain (*peninsulares*) to get appointments to these high offices, with lesser positions, such as county presidents (*alcaldes mayores*) or regional commanders (*corregidores*) to be staffed with creoles (persons of Spanish descent born in the New World). These high-ranking officials formed a bureaucratic corps separate from the creole landholders, although some of these officials ultimately became founders of important creole families. Although the Viceroy of New Spain nominally had jurisdiction over the Kingdom of Guatemala, in practice, because its officials could communicate directly with the royal government in Spain, they often bypassed the Viceroy. Yet there were enough instances in which the viceroys intervened in the Kingdom's affairs to create some feelings of antagonism toward Mexico City among Guatemalans. Guatemalan merchants also resented the superior trade privileges and opportunities that the Mexican elite enjoyed. In the indigenous villages, of course, caciques often remained in control, effectively collaborating with the Spanish bureaucracy and thereby protecting themselves against the ambitions of creole landholding and commercial interests.

The Church actively joined the State in establishing Spanish civilization in Guatemala. The clergy came to convert and instruct the indigenous population and to minister to the settlers, the Diocese of Guatemala being formally established in 1534. Dedicated missionaries like Bartolomé de las Casas tempered the brutal aspects of the Conquest as they installed the institutions of Christianity. The Bishop of Guatemala became a powerful partner to the Captain General of Guatemala, although Church-State relations were not always cordial. The Church was the agent of an official royal policy of humane treatment of the natives, a role that often led it into conflict with civil officials and settlers. Yet there were many cases where Church and State worked together harmoniously. Bishop Marroquín, Bishop of Guatemala from 1533 to 1563, for example, provided inspired leadership for the Church as well as for the city of Santiago during its difficult early years.

The religious orders were vital in controlling the indigenous population. By 1600 there were twenty-two Franciscan, fourteen Dominican, and six Mercederian convents in Guatemala. The Jesuits arrived in 1582 and they, too, played an important role in education and in agricultural production, especially of sugar. The Jesuits were more aggressive than the other orders, and their efforts to start schools and increase their properties often earned them the jealousy of other clergy. Both the monastic orders and the secular clergy acquired considerable wealth, contributing to some resentment toward the clergy on economic grounds. They ran large estates, served as bankers, and even constructed roads and bridges. Church power grew in the seventeenth century with the construction of many new churches, basilicas, monasteries, and charitable institutions. Also opened, in 1681, under Church auspices was the University of San Carlos de Guatemala. These buildings helped to make Santiago (Antigua) one of America's loveliest cities. By 1700 it ranked only behind Mexico City and Lima in size and importance.

The Bethlehemite Order originated in Guatemala, blossoming from the work and devotion of the Franciscan friar, Pedro de San José de Betancurt during the years 1651–1667. Betancurt came to Guatemala from the Canary Islands and devoted himself to the care of the poor and sick. In his last testament, he called on his followers to form a brotherhood to maintain his hospital in Guatemala. His principal disciple, Rodrigo de la Cruz (formerly Rodrigo Arias Maldonado, Marquis of Talamanca and Interim Governor of Cost Rica), in 1668 organized the Bethlehemite Order, which gained papal confirmation in 1672. Viewed unenthusiastically by the Spanish government, this order remained small until the eighteenth century, but by the end of the colonial era, it had seventeen hospitals throughout Spanish America and one in the Canaries, as well as several schools. This lone male religious order to originate in Spanish America did not survive the anticlericalism of the nineteenth century, although a small female branch, organized in 1670, continues to exist. In the summer of 2002 Pope John Paul II proclaimed sainthood for Betancurt during his third visit to Guatemala. There is a shrine to Saint Pedro de Betancurt at the Church of San Francisco in Antigua Guatemala.

Santo Hermano Pedro de San José de Betancurt, in the background San Francisco el Grande Church

Despite the clergy's zeal in Christianizing the indigenous population, the principal motivation for colonization of Guatemala was economic. The hope for easy wealth, preferably gold or silver, attracted Spaniards to the country and the availability of indigenous labor to build agricultural estates kept them there after mining proved less lucrative than they had hoped. Agriculture came to be the mainstay of its economy. Landholding was the key to social and economic security and advancement within a framework of Spanish feudalism. Royal decrees confirming the land grants by conquistadors and granting new lands to later arrivals created the foundation for the dominant families who would rule the country for centuries.

Essential to the power of landholding was labor to work the land. Forced labor characterized the colonial system from the beginning. The Spaniards required the indigenous peoples to pay tribute and forced them to work in order to make the tribute payments. Although the Crown abolished Indian slavery early, it was replaced by the enduring institution of the *encomienda*, which granted landholders the labor of Indians from nearby villages to work their lands. The New Laws of 1542 formally abolished the encomienda system, but lax enforcement and evasion allowed the system to continue in Guatemala well into the seventeenth century, when it gave way to another practice that allowed exploitation of Indian labor to continue, the *repartimiento*.

The repartimiento required indigenous men between ages 16 and 60, excepting only caciques and those who were ill, to work so many days of the month for landholders, religious, municipalities, or government institutions. In practice, the Audiencia assigned a quarter of the men of each village each week, but additional days were often spent in traveling to and from the place of assignment. The law required that the Indians be paid, usually one *real* (one-eighth of a peso or dollar) per day, but in practice little money changed hands, for the employers "charged" the Indians for what they consumed. The repartimiento evolved into debt slavery in the eighteenth and nineteenth centuries. Under this system some Indians moved into larger towns, but traditionally indigenous communities survived and some became quite large including Quetzaltenango, Totonicapán, Cobán, Momostenango, Santa Cruz del Quiché, Sololá, and Escuintla.

Subsistence agriculture or production of foodstuffs for the local market occupied most of the people, yet export commodities eventually came to dominate the economy. Cacao had grown along the Pacific slopes of Guatemala in pre-Columbian times and became an important early export in Spanish Guatemala, overcoming the objections of some priests who claimed that chocolate was a dangerous drug. Later, indigo was important. Grown mostly in what is today El Salvador, Guatemala City merchants financed and exported the blue dye that was so important to the emerging textile industries of Europe. The relative lack of importance of Guatemalan production for international trade after 1550 meant that the kingdom became something of a backwater in the Empire, overshadowed by the precious metal production of Peru and Mexico. Most farmers produced livestock, corn, wheat, and other crops for the local residents. Some indigenous communities, especially in the heavily-populated valleys near the capital, specialized in food production. Sugar plantations, worked by African slaves, arose around Lake Amatitlán as well as in the Verapaz and elsewhere. The Spaniards, as well as many ladinos, depended upon the Indians for their food. Indigenous traders brought the produce into the urban markets. Such markets remain today an integral aspect of Guatemala life.

There was little manufacturing beyond essential items in colonial Guatemala. Spain itself lagged behind other European nations in manufacturing and it discouraged colonial factories that would compete either with Spanish production or with the foreign goods that its merchants carried. Inevitably, because of the high cost of transporting European goods to Guatemala, local production of some goods, especially clothing, leather goods, housewares, and other everyday necessities of course occurred. Municipal regulations closely regulated the quality and prices of such goods. Shoemakers, tailors, and other craftsmen organized into guilds aimed at limiting competition and maintaining standards, but they rarely sold their goods beyond the local area. Local traders, on the other hand, carried indigenous textiles, pottery, crude furniture, etc. to native markets throughout the country. The Spanish elite, insisting on European finery, shunned these native-made goods, but they gained acceptance among middle and lower class Guatemalans. Imported goods commanded prices that only the well-to-do could afford, while the vast majority of the population used locally-made goods. Price controls provided some check against runaway inflation for scarce goods, while the exploitive labor system kept wages low. There was a shortage of currency to such an extent that barter was widespread. Establishment of a Guatemalan mint in 1731 improved that situation somewhat, although credit continued to be difficult and interest rates were high. Clergy often played the role of bankers, although merchants also extended credit to planters against future crops.

Poor communications, exacerbated by the rugged terrain, heavy rains, and frequent earthquakes and landslides, retarded commercial development and production. Guatemala's ports were small and underdeveloped on the unhealthy lowland tropical coasts. Disease, the jungle, the climate, floods, and landslides all worked against repeated efforts to develop a Caribbean port. Although Spain had opened the port of Santo Tomás de Castilla in 1604, it had not prospered and only a small amount of trade trickled through the Gulf of Honduras.

Colonial Guatemalan society consisted of three recognizable classes, plus several other more mobile sectors. The majority of the population consisted of indigenous serfs plus a few African slaves. This laboring class tilled the fields and provided personal service to the Europeans. Their masters made up the other two classes, much smaller in size but with elite status. First were the Spanish bureaucracy, residing principally in Santiago. Mostly Spanish-born (*peninsulares*) and, except for the justices of the Audiencia, temporary residents who carried out their duties in service to the Crown and themselves, they had little interest in the long-term prosperity of the Kingdom of Guatemala. The second elite class were large landholders, most of whom had been born in the colony (creoles), essentially a kind of colonial aristocracy, although few ever held noble titles. Denied easy access to the high administrative offices or control of the powerful institutions because of the monopolization of these institutions by the bureaucratic class, this ever-expanding creole class found strength in its control of production and commerce. These creoles often exercised considerable influence through evasion of laws, corruption, and smuggling. Some peninsular bureaucrats, of course, became founders of creole families, and new settlers arrived throughout the colonial period so that there were always some Spanish-born among the "creole aristocracy."

The combination of its economic power with the moral pressure of the Catholic clergy created a paternalistic attitude among this landholding class. Many of the Indians persisted in their pre-conquest religious beliefs in a kind of natural defense against Spanish-Christian cultural imperialism. Such pagan manifestations even today are easily found among indigenous Guatemalans. The Guatemalan creole mentality rationalized that the Indians lived happily in their poverty, arguing that the legal serfdom of the Indians was necessary because without such requirements the Indians would not work at all. In creole eyes the Indian was inclined to vice and drunkenness, which would increase unless they were kept occupied with obligatory labor.

Race mixture occurred from the beginning and a growing number of *ladinos* populated the towns and countryside. These offsprings of Spaniards and Indians did not always win ready acceptance into either creole or peninsular society, although by the eighteenth century creole society included many ladinos. Some ladinos worked as rural wage laborers, and some held small farms, entered commerce, or even the professions. A much larger number formed a classless group in the major towns. From their ranks came artisans, small merchants, peddlers, service personnel, etc., to form a middle sector of considerable importance in Guatemalan society.

While there was much accommodation and collaboration between the peninsular officialdom and the creole elite, the Audiencia best represented the peninsular, imperial interests, whereas the city councils (*ayuntamientos*, or *cabildos*), largely composed of creoles, represented local interests. These institutions clashed over control of wealth and Indians as well as over petty, personal differences, as each group jealously guarded its privileges and status. By the eighteenth century differences between the two classes were significant and were leading to rising animosity. Both of the upper classes abused and exploited the indigenous masses, as did also the urban middle sectors. There were, for example, middlemen who supplied foodstuffs and other goods for the towns and they often dealt harshly and brutally with their indigenous suppliers, seeking to get the lowest possible prices. At the bottom of the social order in spite of lengthy royal decrees offering protection and devoted clergy who championed their interests at times, the indigenous peoples were always subject to intimidation, harassment, and cheating.

If the elite of Santiago de Guatemala paled in comparison to that of Mexico or Lima, there was nonetheless sufficient wealth to encourage considerable beautification of the capital city. By the eighteenth century Santiago had magnificent homes and large commercial houses near the center of the city, but the city's grandeur was most evident in the opulence of its great churches, monasteries, convents, and seminaries. An architectural style developed in Santiago that smaller towns throughout the kingdom imitated.

Ruins of La Recolección Church and Monastery in Antigua Guatemala, destroyed by the 1773 earthquake

Courtesy of Janice Chatelain Woodward, 2005

City Hall Palace (Ayuntamiento), Antigua Guatemala

Courtesy of Janice Chatelain Woodward, 2005

Palace of the Captains General, Antigua Guatemala

Courtesy of Janice Chatelain Woodward, 2005

Ultimately, Spain's colonial policies and European wars drained valuable resources from Guatemala. The Crown called on the American dominions unceasingly for financial support. In the seventeenth century rising taxation, forced loans, and other assessments increased the burden on the colonial economy. Widespread tax evasion and corruption came to be a major part of the colonial economic life, a situation persisting to the present. Supervision over every aspect of the economy was detailed and restrictive, but not necessarily inflexible. Bribery and other forms of corruption was the creole answer to Spanish regulations. Depression and currency depreciation contributed to a real decline in living standards in the latter part of the seventeenth century, but government officials supplemented their salaries with the illicit activities and bribes, and they frequently ignored royal prohibitions against engaging in commerce or other private remunerative activities.

Smuggling, in fact, as in other parts of the Spanish Empire, was common. The French, Dutch, and English all brought less expensive goods to Central America in exchange for cacao, tobacco, indigo, and other plantation crops, as well as for the Spanish pieces of eight (precursor of the U.S. dollar). Lax enforcement and the willingness of royal officials to accept bribes or other payoffs permitted smugglers to flourish. There were also raids on both the Caribbean and Pacific shores by enemy naval forces or by lawless buccaneers. Spain raised great fortresses in defense, but the forts did not always stop the invaders. Fort San Felipe, on the Río Dulce, stands today as a reminder of those swashbuckling days.

As early as 1638 British loggers began to move onto the Guatemalan coast in what is today Belize. Among the early buccaneers there was one Peter Wallace and the name Belize is actually a Spanish corruption of his name. Spain refused to recognize British sovereignty there and occasionally its naval forces succeeded in dislodging the intruders, but by the 1660s the settlement operated as an informal British colony. Other buccaneers operated further down the coast as far as Panama and eventually established a British presence in Honduras's Bay Islands and on Nicaragua's Miskito Coast.

By 1700 Guatemala had become a well-established Spanish kingdom with an entrenched landholding class that would defend with vigor its privileges and property. The Maya culture of pre-Columbian days survived in Guatemala alongside the European elites, but there was no assimilation into a homogenous society. The eighteenth century would bring great change to both the culture and economy of the country, but a deep legacy of Habsburg rule remained in Guatemala's political tradition.

3

Independence

Pedro Molina

In 1700 Spain's impotent Habsburg King, Carlos II, finally died after a quarter century of hapless rule during which Spanish power and prestige declined notably. Succeeding to his throne was Carlos's grandnephew and second cousin, the Bourbon Felipe V, a grandson of Louis XIV of France. Ths event triggered the costly War of the Spanish Succession (1701–1714). This and subsequent intercolonial wars throughout the century directly shaped Guatemalan history, leading eventually to national independence more than a century later. These conflicts produced profound challenges to the status quo in the eighteenth century. French and English ideas penetrated the Spanish empire, contributing to a revolution in mentality in Guatemala that was part of the larger intellectual revolution known as the Enlightenment. Modern Guatemala, in many ways, dates from the late eighteenth century.

The Spanish Bourbons decreed French-inspired reforms that touched many aspects of life in Guatemala and stimulated changing thought and action among Guatemalan creoles. These policies fell into four types: 1) anticlerical reforms designed to reduce the size and political influence of the clergy, 2) commercial and economic reforms designed to increase Spanish trade and government revenues, 3) administrative reforms designed to provide more efficient government and to improve tax collection, and 4) military and naval measures to improve Spain's defense and protect her commerce. All of these reforms had the larger goal of restoring Spanish prestige, prosperity, and authority in a century that found a once-great empire reduced to a second-rate position behind Britain and France.

The most important changes occurred in Guatemala during the reigns of Carlos III (1759–1788) and Carlos IV (1788–1808), although there were some significant reforms earlier in the century. Guatemala had been a leading center of ecclesiastical power and prestige in Central America. The Dominican estates in the Verapaz made it the richest order in the Kingdom, but the Franciscans were an impressive second, and others also had significant wealth, including the Jesuits. The Bourbons began to restrict the power of the clergy early in the century. Royal decrees limited the right of religious orders to construct new monasteries or to accept novices prior to adulthood. The Crown lowered or abolished certain taxes that supported the Church, not to destroy the Church, but to reduce the power of the orders and to bring the Church more definitely under the reign of the State. These reforms were aimed more especially at the religious orders than at the secular clergy hierarchy, which the Crown supported in what it deemed legitimate activities. Thus in 1743, for example, Guatemala became an Archdiocese, with jurisdiction over the entire Kingdom. The most well-known anticlerical reform, of course, was the expulsion of the Jesuit Order from the Spanish Empire in 1767. In Guatemala, other orders took over the Jesuit enterprises, but in many ways the loss of these industrious clergy was costly to the kingdom.

Administrative reorganization of the Spanish Empire into a more modern ministerial system began in 1705. Making colonial administration more efficient would eventually touch the lives of Guatemalans. Welcome increases in salaries, aimed at encouraging incentives and promoting more responsible officials contributed to improvement in both the quality of personnel and in their services by the final third of the eighteenth century, but inflation limited the economic value of many of these gains and in turn encouraged graft and corruption. Creoles found their way into administrative offices at a more rapid pace than before. There was a more conscious effort to build infrastructure and promote economic development in Guatemala. The establishment of a royal mint in Guatemala City in 1731, for example, helped ease the chronic shortage of currency.

International rivalry prompted some of the most important commercial and military modifications. The British had made inroads all along the eastern coast of Central America, on the Miskito coast, on the Bay Islands, and at Belize, which had become a haven for significant contraband trade with Guatemala, as well as a major British source for mahogany and dyewoods. The Spanish occasionally dislodged the Belize woodcutters, but they always returned. By 1741 British officials in Jamaica regularly appointed a Superintendent for Belize, although for the most part the local inhabitants managed their own affairs. In 1754 the Spanish sent 1500 troops through the Petén, but 250 British defended Belize against the invasion and increased their hold on that region during the subsequent Seven Years' War (1756–1763) when British naval forces dealt catastrophic blows to Spanish shipping in Central American waters. By the Treaty of Paris of 1763 Britain recognized Spanish sovereignty over Belize and agreed to dismantle her fortifications there, but in return Spain had to allow the English to continue to settle there and to cut dyewood. In fact, the British did not dismantle the fortifications. The British colonies remained, and Belize continued as a self-governing outpost of British imperialism and a major port for smuggling with Guatemala.

Spain attempted to regain the trade lost to France and Great Britain by dismantling the trade monopoly that the Andalusian ports of Seville and Cádiz had held over the American trade. Without discarding the principal of monopoly itself, the Spanish Bourbons opened participation in its closed commercial system to a wider number of Spaniards and colonists in an effort to offer alternatives to smuggling. Earlier in the century authorization of private trading companies to trade directly between Spain and Honduras and Guatemala had failed for lack of sufficient capital and infrastructure, but they were a step toward freer commerce. After 1763 the government of Carlos III took more aggressive steps, culminating in the Free Trade Act of 1778, which greatly expanded opportunities for Central Americans to engage directly in trade with both Spain and other colonies. The roads and ports of Guatemala were ill suited for these new opportunities, but colonial governors urged the Church, the military, and other institutions to accelerate road-building and navigation of the Motagua and Polochic Rivers. The volume of trade increased notably. Sonsonate, as a center of the indigo-producing region on the Pacific shore, enjoyed the greatest growth, regaining the prominence it had once held as a cacao center. In 1803 the Pacific coast ports were allowed to receive re-exported Asian goods by sea from Acapulco. Meanwhile, regular mail ship service between Spain and Guatemala began in 1764.

The rising commerce promoted the emergence of a larger and more vocal merchant community in Guatemala City. The Free Trade Act of 1778 had authorized establishment of new merchant guilds (*consulados de comercio*), giving merchants their own commercial court and an institution for the protection and development of commerce, a privilege only the merchants of Mexico and Lima had enjoyed previously in Spanish America. Guatemala, in 1793, was the second of eight additional Spanish-American cities to receive permission to establish such an institution. Surviving well beyond independence, Guatemala's Consulado became an important court for commercial litigation and the principal builder of roads, bridges, ports, and other infrastructure in Guatemala until 1871. Other Bourbon reforms placed alcohol and tobacco under state control—not to limit consumption, but to keep these items out of the contraband trade and to increase government revenues from their sales.

Imitating earlier French models, the Spanish in 1786 appointed superintendents (*intendentes*) to oversee financial and military administration in the Kingdom of Guatemala. The Crown appointed superintendents for Honduras, El Salvador, Nicaragua, and Chiapas. Guatemala itself remained outside the system, under the direct administration of the Captain General in the capital, but this new system established El Salvador as separate from the Province of Guatemala, removing it from the direct administration of Guatemala. As the superintendents held broad financial and military authority, this new organization increased provincial autonomy and thus contributed to the separatist spirit of the outlying provinces. Salvadoran nationalism essentially dates from the start of the intendancy system and would lead to considerable enmity toward Guatemala during the next century.

Military buildup and reorganization during the American Revolution (1775–1783) increased the number of regular Spanish troops in Central America, but a more important change was the enlargement of local reserve militias, which eventually became the nucleus later for the national armies in the Central American states.

Despite some increase in production and exports stimulated by the freer trade policies, several factors combined to depress the Guatemalan economy in the late eighteenth century. Serious upheaval had literally begun with a series of devastating earthquakes in 1773 that destroyed the city of Santiago, leading to a decision to move the capital to a new site in the Valle de la Hermita, some 50 kilometers away. Although not all the inhabitants left the old city (Antigua Guatemala), the government tried to force everyone to leave and put a major effort into the construction of the new capital (Nueva Guatemala). Some of the residents, however, preferred to move to more settled areas, especially around Quetzaltenango, which also enjoyed significant growth as a result of the catastrophe at Antigua. A further difficulty was a serious smallpox epidemic in 1780. Vaccinations, given here for the first time in Guatemala, helped stem this epidemic.

While the new construction stimulated economic growth that to some degree offset the disruption caused by the earthquake, international factors also contributed to the economic depression of the late colonial period. Exports of cacao and other products declined as other producers in areas more accessible to the Atlantic commerce emerged. The Guatemalan merchants had encouraged and financed production of indigo in El Salvador. It had offered some recovery following the decline of cacao exports, but competition from other producers in Venezuela and South Carolina and a series of locust invasions caused Central American production to drop sharply during the final two decades of the colonial period. Production dipped from nearly a million pounds of the dye between 1791 and 1800 to less then half that amount between 1810 and 1820. Given the hard times and a growing presence of the British on the Caribbean shores, it is not surprising that there was a rise in smuggling and contraband activities, both of which encouraged the notion that free trade was advantageous and would bring lower prices for foreign goods. Moreover, the Spanish military and naval buildup required higher taxes, forced loans, so-called "patriotic donations" to the government, and alarming inflation, all of which added to the costly process of building the new capital city.

Spanish involvement in the American Revolution had direct repercussions in Guatemala. Spain did not formally enter the conflict in alliance with France against Britain until 1779, but there had already been growing friction with the British all along the eastern coast. Upon the declaration of war in 1779 Spanish forces attacked and drove the English from Belize and Roatán (in Honduras's Bay Islands), but most of those settlers simply moved to the Miskito Coast. Guatemala's Captain General, Matías de Gálvez, countered with a campaign that repelled the British attempt to cut the Spanish Empire in half at Nicaragua. The Peace of Paris (1783) ending the war reaffirmed the earlier treaty, confirming Spanish sovereignty on the eastern coast. But a revision of the Treaty in 1786 once more allowed the British to settle and cut dyewood and mahogany at Belize and it allowed the British from the Miskito Coast to return to Belize. From that point on, Belize thrived as a center for extensive commerce with Guatemala.

Subsequently, Spain become embroiled in the wars arising from the French Revolution. First, it joined Britain and other European monarchies in the attempt to overturn the French Republic. Then, in 1796, the French, after several military victories, forced Spain to switch sides and ally with France against England. British control of the sea from that point forward cut Spain off from her American dominions and forced her to allow them to trade with foreigners. Spain now essentially lost economic control of Guatemala and there suddenly was a rising trade with the United States, the leading neutral in these wars until 1812.

The Bourbon reforms, changing fortunes in the international trade of Guatemalan commodities, and the demands of war thus brought substantial change to Guatemala. The landholding elite reacted cautiously. Some of them had been influenced by the intellectual currents of the Enlightenment and there was a developing liberal element among them. Yet many of the wealthiest creoles did not believe that the Bourbon Reforms necessarily improved their lot in the Kingdom of Guatemala. In fact, the reforms that sought more efficient administration often challenged the accommodation of corruption and evasion that the creoles had developed with the bureaucracy. There had been riots and revolts in opposition to the establishment of liquor and tobacco monopolies, and the increased demands on Indian labor that came from the Crown's emphasis on greater productivity had been answered with revolts in some indigenous towns after 1760. None were so great as to threaten the stability of the kingdom as was the case with the Tupac Amaru revolt in Peru (1780–1783), the Comunero revolts in New Granada (1781), or the Hidalgo revolt in Mexico (1810), but they nonetheless reflected a growing restlessness and fear over the changes taking place at various levels of the society. Economic hard times and the tightening of Spanish administrative control at the close of the eighteenth century heightened the tensions between the bureaucracy and the creole elite, as well as the rivalry between the capital and the outlying provinces.

Notable change was occurring among the creole elite. Old families, dating from the sixteenth-century Conquest, formed a conservative core that resisted change. But an increase in European immigration under the stimulus of the Bourbon reforms brought more aggressive and more liberal individuals, many from the Basque provinces, to Guatemala in the late eighteenth century. A few of these newcomers had phenomenal economic success and began to assume leadership of a more progressive element of the elite. The rise to prominence of the house of Aycinena is the best example of this phenomenon. Juan Fermín de Aycinena came to Guatemala in 1754. A native of Navarra, he had profited in Mexico as a muleteer and then reinvested his profits in indigo and livestock in Guatemala and El Salvador. He also invested in Honduran silver mining, but indigo became his principal economic activity and he established an important exporting house in the new capital of Guatemala. In 1780 he purchased the title of Marquis from the government of Carlos III and became the only resident holder of a noble title in the Kingdom at that time. The Marquis de Aycinena soon became the leader of the Guatemalan elite, a process probably facilitated by the disruption caused by the destruction of the capital as well as the other upsetting events of the period, but perhaps even more by his three successive marriages into prominent Guatemala landholding and commercial families (Carrillo Gálvez, Nájera Mencos, and Piñol Muñoz). So well woven into the fabric of upper-crust Guatemalan society did the Aycinenas become, that the elite came to be known by its enemies simply as "the family."

Many Guatemalan creoles by the close of the eighteenth century had developed a negative attitude toward Bourbon Spain. While they often idealized a glorious Spanish past—Spain at the peak of its power, the Spain of the Conquest, with its elevated cultural and spiritual values reflected in the literature of the "Siglo de Oro"—they viewed themselves as defenders of that spirit in the New World, and they viewed the royal officials with whom they had to deal with mistrust and suspicion. For them the Bourbon Reforms threatened their economic and political positions with bothersome and misguided laws. Moreover, ambitious new immigrants challenged their share of the land and wealth of the colony. The creole elite developed an intuitive bitterness and was forming a conservative core that would survive to the present. In that creole mentality, the Indian was a beast of burden who could be treated with animal brutality in order to preserve society. The creoles supported the government in suppressing indigenous communities that resisted the increased labor demands and efforts to seize their lands. An authentic indigenous civilization persisted widely in the western highlands. There, Indians continued to speak native Mayan dialects and to live outside the mainstream of Hispanicized Guatemala.

Meanwhile, the ladino population had become the backbone of the middle sectors. The growth of wage labor and debt peonage provided opportunities for ladinos both to work as laborers for the elite classes and serve as middlemen between rural Indian food producers and the urban populations. Some Indians migrated into urban areas and took on Hispanic characteristics and thus become ladinos. Ladinos dominated the artisan class, providing goods and services for the elite. An upper middle sector dominated the profession, but also served the elite. At the bottom of the urban middle sector was an underemployed urban rabble. But the indigenous population remained the majority and the creole class guarded its social and economic privileges against ladino ambition.

Amid rising discussions of these political and economic reforms, Spain's colonial empire began to disintegrate in the face of British imperialism. Losses in the American Revolution had been a temporary setback for the British, but the Napoleonic wars were devastating to Spain's control of Central America and the rest of the empire. Britain had retaken the Bay Islands and successfully repulsed a Spanish attack on Belize in 1798. Skirmishes continued into the first decade of the new century as the British extended their influence on Nicaragua's Miskito Coast. After Napoleon invaded Spain and placed his brother, Joseph Bonaparte, on the Spanish throne in 1808, a Spanish resistance movement allied with Great Britain in 1809. Thereafter Guatemalan trade with Britain expanded rapidly. Belize, as the entrepôt for this trade, with a population of less than 5,000, took on a more prosperous appearance. The sudden flow of British goods into Guatemala not only finished off the Spanish trade monopoly, but also damaged the limited manufacturing, particularly of textiles, that Spain permitted in Guatemala, as an ever-increasing supply of comparatively inexpensive British goods poured into the country. As a by-product, British economic and political ideas also penetrated more readily.

Guatemala had its first printing press by 1660, and its first newspaper appeared briefly in 1729–1731, but until the late eighteenth century religious tracts and government proclamations accounted for most publication. By 1800, however, foreign ideas had challenged the order that Spain had established over nearly three centuries. Some members of both the bureaucracy and the creole elite had begun to favor freer economic institutions, representative government, and a more open political process, and some questioned the wisdom of monopolies, special privilege, and the traditional role of the Church. Conservatives resisted these new ideas, but by 1810 there were individuals throughout the Kingdom of Guatemala who represented an enlightened sector of the Guatemalan elite. These included a Costa Rican friar, José Antonio Liendo y Goicoechea, who championed curriculum reform in the university; a Honduran lawyer, José Cecilio del Valle, who promoted the study of political economy in the colony; two dynamic editors of the liberal and sometimes controversial *Gazeta de Guatemala* —Alejandro Ramírez and Simón Bergaño y Villegas; the publisher of the *Gazeta*, Ignacio Beteta; a Salvadoran planter-merchant, Juan Bautista Irisarri, who advocated freer trade and port construction on the Pacific Coast; and a leading cleric, Father Antonio García Redondo, who argued for giving ladinos greater economic opportunity to increase agricultural production. These men formed the nucleus of the Economic Society (*Sociedad Económica*) of Guatemala, an institution similar to the Philosophical Societies in the English-Speaking world that had originated in Switzerland in the mid-eighteenth century, spread across France and into Spain, and on to Spanish America in the 1790s. Founded in Guatemala in 1795, it promoted ways to improve the economy, the arts, education, and industry. It supported the new newspaper, *Gazeta de Guatemala,* and sponsored classes in political economy, bookkeeping, mathematics, foreign languages, and drafting when the University failed to offer such modern subjects. Its

José Cecilio del Valle

liberalism led the government to suppress it in 1800, but it began again in 1811 under the more liberal government of the Spanish resistance parliament (*Cortes*) at Cádiz and undoubtedly was an influence in changing the mentality of many members of the elite. There now existed a significant number of people who looked forward to change and progress.

The promulgation of the Constitution of 1812 by the Cortes of Cádiz reflected the emerging differences between Liberals and Conservatives throughout the Empire, and it established the political dialogue for the half-century to follow in the Spanish world. The liberal Spanish Cortes (1810–1814) restored the Guatemalan Economic Society, created three legislative councils (*Diputaciones Provinciales*)—for Guatemala, León (Nicaragua), and Ciudad Real (Chiapas)—and provided for the election of ayuntamientos, establishment of a new University at León, and liberalization of trade. Central Americans played prominent roles in the Cortes, as representatives from all six provinces were among the signers of the 1812 Constitution, including Guatemala's Antonio Larrazábal.

Self interest and rivalry with the colonial bureaucracy, rather than a truly progressive spirit, guided the Central American delegates to the Cortes of Cádiz. For the moment, however, they championed political liberalism, elective and representatives offices, a relaxation of commercial restrictions, efforts to stimulate production and develop intellectual as well as economic resources, a freer press, and the emergence of incipient political parties. In the 1810 elections the elite maintained control of the Guatemala City government and of the newly created legislative council, but Larrazábal no sooner left for Spain than a change of command in Guatemala led to a reactionary turn in the political climate of the kingdom.

The new Govenor, Captain General José de Bustamante y Guerra, arrived on 14 March 1811, following a successful command at Montevideo where he had effectively resisted the creole elite of Buenos Aires. A man of singular dedication to duty and unswerving loyalty to the Crown as well as to the principles of authority and absolutism, Bustamante had little sympathy with the liberal Cortes or the Constitution and much less with the ambitious creole elite headed by the Aycinenas. While enforcing the letter of the liberal laws of the Cortes, he displayed a notable lack of compliance with their spirit. He censored the press and stifled the creole ayuntamientos and legislative councils. He curtailed foreign trade in his zeal for stopping smuggling, and he was obviously delighted when the restored Bourbon, Fernando VII, suppressed not only the Constitution, but all the decrees of the Cádiz government, in a decree of 4 May 1814, which Bustamante published in Guatemala on 19 August.

Larrazábal now found himself in a Spanish jail. Bustamante was especially hard on the powerful Aycinena clan, who had been vocal in their support of the liberal policies of the Cádiz government. A group of pro-Spanish merchants in the capital now had the ear of the Captain General. Bustamante sought ways to increase productivity and thereby reverse the declining economic trends and spreading poverty, but his proposals for land distribution and salaried labor, giving landless Indians and ladinos small plots, merely alienated further the creole aristocracy against him. For them his projects were a threat to their own land and labor. Economic benefits to the creole aristocracy declined in direct correlation to their political status. Bustamante refused them positions of high office, pressed a suit for back taxes against the Aycinena family, and denied them government protection, an advantage they had formally enjoyed. Some turned to contraband trade. A few had involved themselves in an abortive plot against Bustamante at the Belén Monastery in December 1813. In January 1814 a new plot in San Salvador also failed dismally. Bustamante clearly suspected the Aycinenas and other creole leaders of revolutionary designs as he guarded against any Central

American imitation of the kind of uprising that Father Miguel Hidalgo had led in Mexico beginning in 1810.

Nevertheless, between 1811 and 1818, while Bustamante suppressed the outward manifestations of political partisanship, political factions crystallized. The differences among the factions were political, social, economic, regional, even religious, but they were not particularly nationalistic or anti-Spanish. There was little open sentiment for independence, and Bustamante's forces easily put down the few isolated insurrections. Supported by the pro-Peninsular merchants in the capital, textile producers, indigo producers, and small landholders throughout the kingdom, the government party defended the protected commercial system. Inexpensive British cottons were a principal target of its policies, as cotton imports were damaging the native weaving industry and cutting into profits traditionally held by the capital's merchants.

Bustamante's hard-line policies left the creole elite in difficult straits. After 1814 their support of the Constitution of 1812 left them ineligible to hold office until 1817 when a general pardon (*indulto*) reinstated their citizenship privileges. But their economic position further deteriorated with declining indigo exports. Then, heavier-than-usual rains in 1816 damaged crops just as the Spanish government imposed a new tax on overseas trade to help defray expenses of an expedition against Simón Bolívar in South America. In Guatemala the elite ultimately found allies among those who shared their hatred of Bustamante—mainly those who favored independence or restoration of the Constitution of 1812. It proved an unlikely alliance of the "best families" with social outcasts, an inordinate number of whom were upper middle sector professionals of illegitimate parentage. This alliance, born of expediency, was doomed to disintegrate once the common enemy was gone in the 1820s. So long as Bustamante remained, the alliance had to be discrete, but the elite had allies elsewhere. Letters flowed from the Aycinenas and others of the "family" to influential friends in Spain, reflecting their desire to see Bustamante relieved.

Relief came in 1818 with the appointment of an elderly, mild-mannered naval officer, Carlos Urrutia y Montoya, as his replacement. The "family" lost no time in courting the new governor and regaining its former position in colonial government. Regardless of the capabilities Urrutia had displayed earlier in his career, by the time he came to Guatemala he was in the twilight of his competence as an administrator. His easygoing style, in fact, permitted a relatively peaceful transition to independence in Central America. While Urrutia harangued against smuggling, his actual decrees made foreign trade easier, for they attempted to replace smuggling with legitimate commerce on which the government could collect taxes. Thus, in 1819 Urrutia authorized legal trade with Belize, and merchants associated with the "family" quickly took advantage of the decree. Meanwhile, privateers supporting rebel governments from Mexico to the Argentine had virtually cleared Spanish trade from the Caribbean, making smuggling even more popular than before.

Then, in 1820, a revolt led by Colonel Rafael Riego among troops at Cádiz awaiting transport to the wars for independence in South America resulted in the restoration of the Constitution of 1812. Suddenly, elections were once more being held. In heavy campaigning, Dr. Pedro Molina in his newspaper, *El Editor Constitucional*, which began publication in July 1820, took up the interests of the Aycinena oligarchy. Molina, of illegitimate birth, was most assuredly not a member of the "family," nor were his close associates. The alliance born in opposition to Bustamante, nevertheless, now formed the basis for opposition to any restrictions on overseas commerce. Free trade became a leading issue, although Molina himself championed independence as well, for even the new liberal Spanish government offered little promise of adequate colonial representation. More moderate elements of the elite responded with their own newspaper, *El Amigo de la*

Patria, edited by José Cecilio del Valle, noted for his liberalism in the late colonial period, but now he was opposing radical change. Del Valle, from a Honduran cattle-ranching family, had come to the capital in the 1790s and made his mark as a successful attorney and government official. Outside the exclusive "family," del Valle, as a leading adviser to Bustamante, had become closely associated with the merchants who opposed the Aycinenas and their relatives. Thus, these two early political factions found members of the upper middle sector as their principal spokesmen. Neither really represented the middle sectors; rather, they stood for different wings of the creole elite, both reflecting the influence of personal interests and Enlightenment thought. The tendency of the Guatemalan elite not to directly run for elected office, but instead to work through middle-sector politicians was a tendency that would only grow stronger over the next two centuries.

These two factions waged passionate campaigns in 1820 for seats on the Guatemala ayuntamiento and the provincial legislative councils. The radicals, called the *Gazistas* or *Bacos* (drunks) by their opponents, charged the moderates, whom they called the *Cacos* (thieves), with corruption, outdated economic views, and self-interest, and they said the moderates were lackeys of the "hated Bustamante." The moderates, retorted with an attack on the elite's privileges and cried out against the dangers of free trade to the jobs of the working-class, especially those engaged in textile production. They defended more gradual, orderly, social and economic reforms consistent with the traditions of the country. In general, the newer members of the elite and the lower classes supported the radicals, while the middle sectors and the older, more well-established families favored the moderates. There was no clear-cut victory for either side, as some candidates elected by the small electorate were not clearly associated with either faction. The moderates gained a slim advantage in the ayuntamiento by virtue of election of José del Valle as First Alcalde, while the radicals gained a narrow margin in the Guatemalan legislative council. Rivalry between these two institutions, which had overlapping functions, added to the difficulties brought on by the partisan politics.

Molina began to press the issue of independence in *El Editor,* whereas the moderate *El Amigo* of Del Valle held to a more loyalist position. In March 1821 Sub-Inspector Gabino Gaínza, recently arrived from Chile, with the support of the legislative council assumed temporary command of the kingdom from the ailing Urrutia. While he issued strong public statements against independence, he privately worked with Molina and the radicals, tolerating if not encouraging independence sentiment. Events in Mexico suddenly forced the issue of independence into Guatemalan politics. On 24 February 1821 Agustín de Iturbide's Plan of Iguala had brought widely differing factions together to establish Mexican independence. News of this Plan traveled southward slowly, but by September there was fear that a Mexican army might be coming to "liberate" Central America. In Chiapas the towns of Comitán, Ciudad Real, and Tuxtla declared for the Plan of Iguala between August 28 and September 5, establishing a precedent for municipalities to decide the issue one by one. In Guatemala City, a council of notables met hastily on 15 September and declared the Kingdom of Guatemala independent. This decision was by no means unanimous, but several moderates had reluctantly accepted independence as an alternative to possible civil war. All of those present representing the Aycinena "family" supported the declaration, which the council adopted by a vote of 23 to 7 in a stormy meeting. It changed practically nothing except political sovereignty. The government remained virtually the same. Moderate leader José del Valle, who had cautioned against the hasty Declaration of Independence, was instrumental in drafting the document and organizing the provisional government, and Gabino Gaínza continued as chief executive.

Having escaped from the Spanish liberal regime, the "family" no longer needed the alliance with Molina and turned instead toward the more conservative del Valle. Thus was born the Conservative Party, although it was not yet called that officially. The immediate issue was not independence from Spain, but rather annexation to Iturbide's Mexican Empire versus an independent republic. The threat of intervention from Mexico influenced the decision, but in the weeks between September and January the nature of the alliance between Molina's pro-independence party and the "family"can be seen vividly. The "family"rapidly consolidated its position and captured key offices. Molina and his close associates received none of them. The transitional nature of the *Gazistas* became evident on this issue. A realignment of factional loyalties took place along more logical class lines. Molina, perhaps somewhat naively, favored complete independence. The creole elite, now led by Mariano Aycinena and his nephew, Juan José, Marquis of Aycinena, ardently championed annexation to royalist Mexico. Following the polling of municipalities throughout the kingdom, the government formally proclaimed annexation on 5 January 1822.

There was violent opposition in some of the provinces to either annexation to Mexico or to rule from Guatemala. The Guatemalan government had quickly established three *comandancias*, with seats of power in Ciudad Real (with jurisdiction over Chiapas and Los Altos), Guatemala (Guatemala and El Salvador), and León (Honduras, Nicaragua, and Costa Rica), following the lines established for the former legislative councils. While the majority of the ayuntamientos of the kingdom approved annexation, there was notable opposition in San Salvador, which had become the leader of the attack on the hegemony of Guatemala City. Troops under the command of a new Captain General from Mexico, Vicente Filísola, finally had to conquer El Salvador in 1823.

With the new alignment of political parties, new labels replaced the earlier ones. The radicals, or liberals, formerly called the *Gazistas* or *Bacos*, now became the *Fiebres* (hotheads). Conservatives or moderates, accused of wanting to continue royalist institutions and of opposing reform, now were dubbed *Serviles* (lackeys), now particularly referring to their domination by the Aycinenas. These terms were borrowed from the contemporary political dialogue in Spain. Membership in and support of these parties first tended to follow the lines established by Molina and del Valle, but as the new economic forces developed—notably free trade and the rise of the cochineal industry—they also reflected the cleavage between Guatemala and the rest of the provinces. The resentment of San Salvador was strongest, and it became the Liberal stronghold, but protests against the economic advantages of the capital came from all the provinces.

Events in Mexico again forced action. The abdication of Iturbide in March 1823 led to a declaration of absolute Central American independence on 1 July of the same year. Only Chiapas chose to remain with Mexico. The other states became the United Provinces of Central America. Because so many of the leading Conservatives were in Mexico City, either as delegates to the imperial Congress or in other government offices, the Liberals were able to take control in Guatemala City. A provisional junta with little authority took over, formed a new government, and suppressed insurgencies in September of 1823. Despite efforts by pro-Spanish elements to overthrow this government, commercial relations with the former mother country and its Cuban colony gradually improved, although Spain withheld formal recognition of the Central American states until after 1850.

Central American independence thus began with political parties that reflected long-standing economic differences. Economic self-interest and jealousies played important roles in the political activities of both factions. Free trade became not just an economic issue, but a political and social one as well, for it threatened the livelihoods of merchants, artisans, and producers who had been protected under the Spanish Empire. At the same time it offered new opportunities for creoles who had held economic, social, and political power and prestige in the days before Bustamante, but which at the hour of independence found themselves struggling in the face of a declining indigo market. To this economic conflict were added political idealism and philosophy stemming from the Enlightenment, still in many ways foreign to the traditions of the region. As a result, the Central American Federation had a turbulent and unstable beginning.

Guatemala's three centuries of colonial rule had imposed durable traditions and patterns on the country. Yet the century preceding independence was a time of great intellectual, economic, and political change. The class structure of Central America reflected these changes as new elements took over leadership of the creole elite and potentially important middle sectors emerged. Spanish rule ended in 1821, but already Great Britain had gained commercial dominance. This set the stage for many of the difficulties of the nineteenth and twentieth centuries.

4

The United Provinces of Central America

Seal of the United Provinces of Central America

Central American independence arrived without the bloody warfare that ravaged much of Latin America. In the decades following the 1821 declaration, however, internal strife split the federation into five small republics, among which Guatemala was by far the largest. Trouble erupted at both state and federal levels over Church-State relations, fiscal policies, office-holding, economic planning, trade policy, and general philosophy of government. Conservatives pleaded for moderation, order, and the stability of traditional institutions. Liberals argued for a continuation of the reforms begun under the Bourbons. The Liberal Party, never very well defined across Central America, had many factions. Often naively idealistic, it sought to make Central America a modern, progressive nation, rejecting its Spanish heritage while eagerly absorbing republican innovations from France, England, and the United States. Liberals challenged the clergy's power and privilege and the monopolistic privileges of other exclusive corporations such as the merchant guild. They favored abolition of slavery, repeal of burdensome taxes on commerce, more egalitarian political and judicial institutions, public education, and road, port, and immigration projects to promote economic development. The Federal Constitution of 1824, patterned somewhat after the United States model of 1789, but more specifically after the Spanish model of 1812, reflected Liberal thought.

The United Provinces never really achieved nationhood, for the provincial jealousies and ideological differences of the late colonial period plagued it from the start. The Constitution granted considerable autonomy to each state, but El Salvador, Honduras, Nicaragua, and Costa Rica all feared Guatemalan dominance. Guatemala's population, estimated at 660,580 in 1825, accounted for more than half the federation's total of 1,288,391 and thus gave Guatemala a preponderant advantage in the federal congress. The early political parties were fluid in composition and family alliances often counted for more than political ideology or class interests. The majority of the population still played little part in politics. Both Liberals and Conservatives represented only factions of the creole elite and upper middle sectors. The scramble for spoils often submerged ideological issue, but the economy remained an important determinant of political affiliation.

After independence, British merchants operating from Belize quickly dominated Guatemalan trade and finance. Advocates of free trade had argued with glowing idealism the economic advantages of independence, yet the rapid introduction of British goods, especially textiles, crippled local industry and threatened local merchants. As these economic realities became evident, leading members of the elite deserted liberalism for more conservative positions.

Almost immediately the form the new government should take led to bitter conflict. Conservatives, especially strong in Guatemala, wanted a centralized state reminiscent of the colonial regime. Liberals, on the other hand, favored a federation on the United States model. The Liberals were stronger in the provinces, where there was strong economic and social resentment toward Guatemala City. The concept of home rule that had developed under the Cádiz Constitution had made deep impressions. An unrealistic optimism infected the Central American Liberals of the 1820s in their prophesies of a prosperous and progressive federation. Their victory in the first national election in 1825 was by only the slimmest of margins, amid cries of fraud. The United Provinces of Central America thus began its existence under a cloud of suspicion, with mistrust among the leaders, and with the extreme Liberals led by José Francisco Barrundia already disenchanted with the new president, the Salvadoran Liberal General Manuel José Arce, whom they accused of making deals with the Guatemalan Conservatives.

José Francisco Barrundia

Even before that election the Liberals had abolished slavery and noble titles, limited the monopolies, enacted a generous immigration law, and ratified the Liberal federal constitution. Now, under the presidency of Arce, they launched a bold revolution that alarmed the Conservatives led by Guatemalan Mariano Aycinena and Honduran José Cecilio del Valle. Tax cuts eliminated many unpopular levies of the Spanish years, but left little revenue to cover the debts that had piled up under Spanish and Mexican rule. To finance expensive new infrastructure projects, Arce's government thus turned to foreign capitalists. It borrowed a large sum from the London firm of Barclay, Herring & Richardson, which after agents' fees, advance interest, and some corrupt skimming, put little cash in the federal treasury. This indebtedness would trouble British-Central American relations for years afterward.

Arce tried to bring order and progress to a federal government that had little real authority over the states. Faced with this situation, he sought a coalition with Guatemala's Conservative elite, who were bristling over Liberal control of the Guatemalan state government under Juan Barrundia, the brother of José Francisco. In collaboration with the Conservatives, Arce deposed Barrundia as Governor of Guatemala, replacing him with Mariano Aycinena. The rest of the Guatemalan state government, led by Lt. Gov. Cirilio Flores, fled first to San Martín Jilotepeque and then to Quetzaltenango, where its legislature enacted such inflammatory liberal laws as declaring children of the clergy legal heirs to Church property, abolishing the Consulado (stronghold of the Conservative merchants), and cutting the tithe tax in half. The Liberals' tenure in Quetzaltenango was short lived, however, for in October a mob attacked Flores, tearing him literally limb from limb, and the Liberal government collapsed. Federal troops under Brigadier Francisco Cáscara, a Sardinian veteran of Napoleon's army, defeated what was left of the state's militia, commanded by Lt. Colonel José Pierson, and reincorporated the western highlands back into Guatemala. Pierson, a creole from Saint Domingue, was another of several foreign soldiers of fortune who served in Guatemala in the early nineteenth century. Captured by the Conservatives, he died before a firing squad on 11 May 1827. Quetzaltenango would remain hostile toward the capital and eventually would become the seat of a secessionist movement aimed at establishing a separate State of Los Altos.

Liberals throughout the provinces reacted violently to Arce's actions. El Salvador was near rebellion over the efforts of Ramón Casáus y Torres, the Conservative Archbishop of Guatemala, to block appointment of Liberal José Matías Delgado as Bishop of El Salvador. El Salvador ultimately seceded from the union, touching off a three-year civil war in 1827. Violence had also flared between Liberal and Conservative factions in Nicaragua. Bitter fighting raged around the Guatemalan-Salvadoran border, and elsewhere, from Los Altos to Costa Rica, skirmishes and revolts brought anarchy and chaos to the isthmus. After initial reverses, the Liberals found a leader in Francisco Morazán, the Honduran son of a creole from the French Caribbean. Morazán's defeat of Guatemalan forces under Generals Justo Milla and Francisco Cáscara at Trinidad, Honduras, on 10–11 November 1827 allowed him to take control of the Honduran government and begin to turn the tide. In the face of these events Arce resigned on 14 February 1828, replaced by his vice president, Guatemalan Conservative Mariano Beltranena.

Arce went into exile and General Manuel Arzú y Delgado de Nájera, founder of Guatemala's first military academy, took over command of the Conservative Army. He launched a new invasion of El Salvador, but in 1828 the Liberals withstood a long siege by the Guatemalans at San Salvador, giving Morazán the opportunity to launch a counter-offensive into Guatemala. Morazán recouped his expenses by imposing forced loans on the conquered Guatemalans as his troops advanced toward the capital. Early in 1829 he restored the Liberal state government at Antigua and then launched a campaign against the capital, which surrendered on 12 April.

Following their victory in 1829, the Liberals dealt vindictively with the Guatemalan elite. Morazán's undisciplined troops looted the city. Morazán jailed the prominent Conservatives until July, when he ordered most of them, including Archbishop Casáus, into exile. He removed priests who had given aid to "enemies of the state," replacing them with "others who have given proof of adhesion to our cause," as both state and federal governments passed strong anticlerical legislation. He granted the state governments extraordinary powers to deal with all who opposed the Liberal regimes.

José Francisco Barrundia served as President of the Federation until an election in June 1830, which failed to give either Morazán or his principal opponent, the moderate José Cecilio del Valle, a majority. Del Valle had not been closely associated with the Aycinenas and the Guatemalan Conservatives since 1826. The Federal Congress was left to decide the election and in September 1830 it chose Morazán, reflecting the Liberal majority in that body. In the years following, Federal President Morazán used the full powers of his office—and more—to attain order and stability in the republic, but in this he failed, for turmoil characterized the following decade. Even after he moved the federal capital from Guatemala to the more sympathetic San Salvador in 1834, he was unable to gain widespread support. Reflecting the disenchantment with Morazán and the Liberals, the presidential election of 1834 went to the moderate del Valle, but he died before taking office. As perhaps the most respected leader on the isthmus, had he lived del Valle might have brought harmony to the opposing forces and thereby preserved the Central American union. In his place, the Congress reelected Morazán, who had apparently been willing to step aside for del Valle. During his second term, however, the rising turmoil in each of the states increasingly occupied Morazán, as they tended to drift away from the federation in their own directions.

The Guatemalan state government was no exception. Its legislature had nullified all acts of Mariano Aycinena's government of 1826–1829 and declared all officers of both the federal and state governments of that period to be traitors. Morazán on 30 April 1829 had reenstated Juan Barrundia to complete his interrupted term as governor, but Barrundia chose not to continue in that position, so the legislature elected Pedro Molina in his stead. Molina irritated Morazán, however, by proposing that the expensive machinery of the federal government be replaced with a Swiss-style federation in which the state governments or the federal congress would hold most of the authority. Morazán fought against this idea and was behind the ouster of Molina by Antonio Rivera Cabezas in March 1830. Rivera had been a powerful writer against the Conservatives as he had ridiculed traditional Hispanic institutions and customs in what had become a sort of cultural revolution by the Liberals. His brief governorship, with most of the Conservatives in exile, ushered in a period of peace in Guatemala. Under his successor, Dr. Mariano Gálvez, the Liberal Revolution in Guatemala reached new heights and laid the ground for the strong reaction against it that broke out in 1837.

Gálvez became Governor in 1831. He pursued strongly Liberal policies, but also brought some measure of harmony back to the country with a policy of conciliation toward the Conservatives, allowing some to return quietly from exile. His economic programs courted middle sector Conservative groups in the capital. An ambitious program to increase production, expand transportation, and colonize lowland areas along the Caribbean coast, for example, promised real benefits to commercial interests, while enactment of protective tariffs appealed to weavers whose markets had been captured by imported British textiles. Although political passions still ran high in the state and there were separatist rumblings from Quetzaltenango, where the inhabitants resented the fact that their voice was small in both state and federal government, by 1834 Gálvez had achieved relative peace in the state. A serious debt, shortage of currency, and accompanying high interest rates still plagued the economy, but cochineal exports, which rose dramatically in the 1830s, gave both planters in the countryside and merchants in the capital a new sense of prosperity. In retrospect, however, Gálvez's first administration was a calm before the storm that soon swept across the state.

A relatively small group of Europeanized residents of Guatemala City dominated the politics of the early national period. Although there was some class mobility, largely along economic and cultural lines, most of the population in the 1830s had little or no voice. Small farmers, merchants, and artisans had suffered greatly from the economic disruption, and rural ladinos came to blame the Liberals for the economic failures. The indigenous majority were more isolated and generally less involved with the European community than were the ladinos. Many indigenous people spoke little or no Spanish. They continued in their traditional way of life, little aware of nor interested in the possibilities of economic or social modernization.

Yet in 1837 a major revolt shattered the delicate atmosphere of conciliation and incipient prosperity. Unlike earlier civil wars, this one did not come from the creoles or upper middle sectors. It erupted instead among the peasant population, especially in the eastern mountain region of Guatemala, the area known as *la montaña*, where a peasant hero, Rafael Carrera, emerged to command the movement. A natural leader, with intuitive military and political insight, Carrera dramatically altered the course of Guatemala history and destroyed Liberal aspirations for more than a quarter-century. Carrera's revolt was not another quarrel between Liberals and Conservative for control of the government. Instead, it was a popular rebellion fueled by rising grievances against the governments of Morazán and Gálvez. This grass-roots reaction against the Liberals also lashed out violently against foreign elements and against efforts to change traditional patterns of rural life.

To the reforms initiated by Spanish Bourbon ministers and accelerated by liberal Spaniards in Napoleonic times, the Guatemalan creoles added a new dimension in their conscious effort to emulate the rapidly advancing English-speaking world. Direct contact with English and North American merchants and diplomats in Central America was responsible for part of this, but probably more important were the readings and travels of Central Americans themselves. Morazán and Gálvez both believed that enlightened legislation could transform Central America into a modern, progressive republic. Believing their nation's underdevelopment to be the results of antiquated Spanish colonialism, they replaced Hispanic institutions and laws with new ones molded upon the experience of Great Britain and the United States. In practice, although they made substantial headway in gaining acceptance among the elite, these changes were not welcome among the lower classes. Gálvez promoted what he believed to be a rational program to improve the state's economy, judicial system, bureaucracy, educational opportunities, communications, and general welfare. But the Guatemalan Liberals displayed exceptional ineptitude in converting a population accustomed to paternalism to their well-intentioned reforms. Many remained unconvinced that Gálvez's program would promote prosperity. The dislocation occasioned by the shift to cochineal production could not easily be absorbed. Gálvez's tariff policies favored the weavers, but heavy imports of British textiles had already ruined many of them, and they continued to be apprehensive of Liberal talk of economic freedom. Cotton production had also dropped for the same reason.

A more immediate cause of the popular uprising was the restoration of a direct head tax, reminiscent of the Spanish tribute abolished shortly after independence. The government had forced loans from wealthy citizens, but this provided inadequate revenue for the ambitious Liberal program. Gálvez established the head tax at two pesos per capita, an amount large enough to be a burden for the Guatemalan peasant of the 1830s. In El Salvador a similar tax had resulted in widespread rioting, forcing suspension of the tax there, but Gálvez maintained it in Guatemala. Gálvez also required enforcement of the obligation of all residents to work on the roads three days out of every month to build the extensive highway network he envisaged. One could substitute a wage payment, but for the masses it meant unwelcome forced labor.

Another Liberal economic program contributing to rural unrest was its land policy. Since 1825 the government had promoted private acquisition of public land in hopes of increasing production. Gálvez accelerated these efforts. This policy allowed those with some capital to increase their holdings. Individual ownership had no great appeal to the Indians, but Gálvez tried to encourage it as a civilizing force. In the end, lands that indigenous inhabitants had formerly used in common passed into the hands of large landholders, and peasants became sharecroppers or debt peons. Large land grants to foreigners stirred unrest especially in eastern Guatemala. Gálvez's program of foreign colonization in the more sparsely inhabited areas sought to stimulate their development and attract a more industrious citizenry into the state. Colonization plans dated from the eighteenth century, but Gálvez's emphasis on colonists from northern Europe was new. British commercial activity out of Belize had intensified the traditional suspicion of foreigners. Spanish colonial administrations had dealt harshly with foreign interlopers, but since independence the Liberals had welcomed them, and this caused apprehension among those who believed themselves to be victims of foreign competition. Concessions made to mahogany loggers and the projects to colonize the northern and eastern portions of the country with Englishmen especially antagonized residents of those regions. They saw the government as more favorable to foreign than to national interests. Such colonization schemes were crucial in turning large numbers of the population toward more traditionalist political leaders and in fueling the Conservative reaction that swept over the isthmus. They cited as evidence of the dangers of such colonization policies the expanding British presence in Belize, the Miskito coast, and the Bay Islands, as well as the secession of Texas from Mexico by Anglo-American colonizers there. Yet the Gálvez government ignored or suppressed petitions against colonization contracts from residents of the region. A rebellion in Chiquimula in the fall of 1835, probably linked to the uprisings in El Salvador against Morazán's federal government, focused on the foreign issue, just as anti-English propaganda inflamed the inhabitants of eastern Guatemala. Government troops put down the rebellion and imposed levies on the towns involved to pay the army's expenses. Such levies were standard practice, but local resentment flared again when the English colonists began to arrive in mid-1836.

Removal of the Roman Catholic clergy from its traditional role in politics, the economy, and education was a major part of the Liberal program that intensified after the Church backed the Guatemala Conservative regime of 1826–1829. In 1829 the Liberals swiftly implemented earlier anticlerical measures and established close control over the Church. Following suppression of monastic orders, exile of prominent Conservative priests, and enactment of religious liberty of the republic, the federal government prevailed upon the Guatemalan government to continue the assault on clerical privilege. They censured ecclesiastical correspondence, seized Church funds and property, stopped collecting the tithe tax, abolished many religious holidays, decreed the right of individual clergy to write their wills as they wished, legitimized the inheritance of parents' property by children of the clergy, authorized civil marriage, and legalized divorce. Priests did not take lightly these challenges to the traditional authority of the Church, especially in the countryside, where parishioners were already disenchanted with the Gálvez government on other grounds. In indigenous and ladino villages the clergy were more than spiritual leaders. They were the most trusted members of the community, and they served as principal advisers to the local authorities. There were often the bankers as well. Given this status, village priests could inflame parishioners against a government that attacked their sacred institution, brought Protestant foreigners into the country, and threatened the very bases of society. Such village priests were the vanguard of the uprising that rocked Guatemala in 1837.

Gálvez also planned to separate education from the Church in favor of public schools open to all Guatemalans. Through a broad range of cultural plans, Gálvez attempted to Europeanize indigenous Guatemalans. One program permitted uneducated children to be taken from their parents and assigned to "protectors" who would provide for their education. In practice, however, this provided inexpensive personal service for the wealthy, and the poorer classes viewed it unfavorably. Understandably, attempts to change long-established customs and prejudices exposed the Gálvez administration to criticism from the illiterate masses as well as from members of the elite who felt threatened by mass education.

Efforts to revise the judicial system reflected well the Liberals' philosophy, but also exposed them to scorn and ridicule. Thoroughly convinced that the Spanish court system was unjust and out of step with enlightened nineteenth-century jurisprudence, the Liberals—led especially by José Francisco Barrundia—adopted legal codes for Guatemala in late 1836 that had been written by Edward Livingston for Louisiana in 1826, but rejected there because they were out of step with Louisiana's French legal traditions. Livingston's codes had received high praise in the English-speaking world and struck the Guatemalan Liberals as a ready replacement for the system they had been abolishing piecemeal. Trial by jury had already been established in 1835. Almost immediately, however, problems had arisen in the countryside. In a state where illiteracy was general and a well-entrenched class structure existed, trial by jury proved impracticable. Anecdotes quickly circulated ridiculing the decisions of indigenous juries. The requirements of Livingston's penal code proved to be equally impracticable, as jails with separate cells for each prisoner did not exist, and their construction with forced labor added to the irritation of the people, who identified the codes much more with centralized rule from Guatemala City, foreign influence, and anticlericalism than with social justice.

Ruthless law enforcement contradicted Liberal claims about liberty and freedom. Police-state measures had been escalating in Guatemala ever since the strong-armed rule of Bustamante, and the Liberals who came to power in 1829 were vengeful against the Conservatives who had preceded them. Gálvez divided Guatemala into four military districts in 1832, and thereafter military government was characteristic. Both Morazán and Gálvez resorted to military solutions in regulating the morality of the inhabitants, suppressing criticism of their own policies, and persecuting their enemies with exile and confiscation of their property. Barbarous conduct by government troops further inflamed country people.

Eastern Guatemala and El Salvador in 1837

From *Rafael Carrera and the Emergence of the Republic of Guatemala, 1821–187,* by Ralph Lee Woodward, Jr. Copyright © 1993 by the University of Georgia Press, p. 63. Used by permssion of the University of Georgia Press.

A terrible cholera epidemic was the catalyst for the 1837 rebellion, even though the epidemic was not unanticipated. After the epidemic had entered Mexico in 1833 Governor Gálvez had warned of its danger to his state. He opened new water and sewage facilities and prohibited burials inside of churches. Despite these precautions, by early 1837 cholera had entered the country, probably through Belize. The government responded by quarantining affected regions, using troops to enforce the quarantines. These measures were sound, but, poorly understood, did not succeed. The rural inhabitants, already alienated from the Gálvez government, feared vaccines, and they believed priests who told them that the chemicals that the government health officers put into the water were poison. Panic resulted in the montaña region. Already disturbed over the Liberal reforms, and believing priestly admonitions that the cholera was a divine punishment on the country, peasants rebelled in various places beginning in March 1837. Although the first insurgency occurred at San Juan Ostuncalco, in Los Altos, more uprisings followed in the eastern montaña.

José Rafael Carrera was a ladino brought up in the poor, Candelaria section of Guatemala City. Lacking formal education, at age14 he was a drummer in the Guatemalan army fighting against Morazán. After the civil war he drifted into the montaña district of Mita and by 1834 had become a swineherd in Mataquescuintla. There a friendly relationship with the village priest led to a favorable marriage into a family of local importance. At the time trouble broke out in 1837 Carrera commanded a platoon of government troops enforcing the cholera quarantines. In June of that year he abandoned his post, responding to a call for aid by peasants resisting government troops in nearby Santa Rosa. Carrera converted a mob of untrained peasants into a fierce guerrilla army. Frequently wounded, this violent man repeatedly displayed exceptional physical courage and determination. Fearlessly leading his forces in fanatical charges against troops with better arms and training, he inspired the peasants to sacrifice, courage, slaughter, and victory.

Popular uprisings against Liberal reforms stretched from Costa Rica to Los Altos in 1837, but the nucleus of the War of la Montaña developed around Carrera in the district of Mita. Carrera's insurgents became a raiding army that forced the government to devote more resources in efforts to stamp it out. Atrocities and vindictive retaliations occurred with rising frequency as the war widened and added to the suffering from the cholera epidemic. In late June Carrera issued a manifesto demanding repeal of the Livingston Codes, protection of life and property, return of the Archbishop and restoration of the religious orders, abolition of the head tax, and amnesty for all those exiled in 1829. He threatened death to any who defied his orders. Government troops often defeated Carrera's guerrillas, but Carrera always eluded capture and found refuge among the peasants of the mountainous country where his legendary image grew steadily.

As the insurgency spread, the Liberals in the capital bickered among themselves. Seeking unity, Gálvez became more conciliatory toward the conservatives, only to alienate the more extreme Liberals. José Francisco Barrundia eloquently attacked the government in the press and in the legislature, accusing Gálvez of suppressing freedom in order to quell a local rebellion. In December Gálvez appointed two Conservatives, Juan José Aycinena and Marcial Zebadúa, as his top ministers, further antagonizing Barrundia. These growing dissensions within the Guatemalan state government caused President Morazán to harbor doubts about Gálvez and he failed to send the military assistance from the federal capital in San Salvador that might have saved the Guatemalan governor.

The military demands of the war raged forced Gálvez to sacrifice most of his reforms for lack of money. Having placed too much faith in advanced laws and too little in popular sentiments, Gálvez now paid the price. Without enough troops to occupy the entire country, Gálvez could not contain the raiding and looting. Moreover, the struggle was becoming a race war, with rural Indians, ladinos, mulattoes, and zambos joining together against the urban white creoles and foreigners. The widespread violence left the countryside thoroughly unsafe. Commerce and communications came to a standstill. Without federal reinforcements, Gálvez's days in office were numbered.

Now Barrundia sought to oust Gálvez. He formed an opposition government at Antigua and entered into an alliance with Carrera, confident that he could dominate the supposedly illiterate guerilla leader. It was a fatal miscalculation. Aycinena and Zebadúa resigned from Gálvez's government. Left alone, Gálvez bravely refused to surrender. He tried to build a larger army and threaten the rebels with attack, but by late January 1838 there was general disaffection with his government even within the capital.

In return for Carrera's military alliance, Barrundia had agreed to nullification of the Livingston codes, relaxation of the anticlericalism, and to recognize Carrera as commander of all insurgent forces. Carrera's peasants swarmed into Guatemala City on the last day of January, 1838. There was some inevitable brutality by the rural forces, but order soon prevailed. Carrera obeyed the new government and kept control of his troops, evacuating most of them within a few days. Barrundia assured him that the Liberal excesses would end. Carrera returned victorious to the montaña, encouraged, according to some sources, by an $11,000 bribe to hasten his departure from the capital.

Barrundia appeared to have triumphed. Gálvez resigned in favor of Lt. Gov. Pedro Valenzuela, much more acceptable to Barrundia. Pedro Molina became president of the legislature. Carrera, commissioned a lieutenant colonel and given military command of his home district of Mita, was out of the capital, along with his dreaded peasant army. Yet the coalition that sustained the government was very fragile. Barrundia lacked a majority in the legislature, where Gálvez still had some support, and the Conservatives now made an important resurgence, having gained first from their alliance with Gálvez and later from the pro-clerical attitude of Carrera. Despite their pro-clerical sentiments, however, they were not yet ready to court the feared guerrilla leader. Thus they vacillated between coalition with moderate Liberals and formation of a new Conservative faction. In the meantime, the departments of Los Altos, taking advantage of the situation, seceded from Guatemala and declared their allegiance to Morazán.

Conservative strength became clear rapidly. By 20 February the government was addressing Carrera as "General." Molina resigned as President of the Legislature. The Church regained its former position. The government called for a return to constitutional rule and ended the military districts. These decrees reflected the popular will as voiced by the guerilla caudillo. The preamble to a decree of 12 March, which terminated all nonelective officeholders, illustrated the attention the legislature gave to this will when it acknowledged that "a great majority of the population of the State have armed themselves to resist the administration that violated their guarantees and the fundamental pact." It justified Carrera's revolt as "directed to re-establishing law and liberty... and demanded by self-preservation against tyranny, [as] not only legitimate but consecrated by reason and justice." The Liberal language of this decree probably reflected the continuing influence of Barrundia, but the repeal of the Livingston Codes soon thereafter indicated his declining power.

Barrundia was slow to recognize the Conservative strength and he doubted Carrera's ability to bring sufficient force against a united government. Carrera, on the other hand, dissatisfied with the government's progress toward his demands, prodded by the anti-government sentiment among rural property holders, and persuaded by the priests advising him that he was being used by the Liberals, renewed guerrilla warfare. Barrundia urged Valenzuela to meet this challenge with military force, but the election of a new Representative Council gave the Conservatives a clear mandate and put Barrundia in an untenable position. Headed by a Conservative, Dr. Mariano Rivera Paz, this Council moved quickly toward accommodation with Carrera. Barrundia appealed once more for help from Morazán, who responded in March with a thousand Salvadoran troops.

Valenzuela had cautioned the federal president against sending troops into Guatemala, for it would upset the recent understanding with Carrera, who had returned to Mita in peace. Morazán now sought to crush the rebellion and restore Liberal power in the state. Carrera responded with new ferocity. Often losing skirmishes, but never decisively defeated, his guerrillas pursued the war in a widening area that stretched from the Caribbean to the Pacific and from El Salvador into the Verapaz and Sacatepéquez. There were atrocities on both sides. Morazán essentially took over the Guatemalan government now, pushing aside the Conservatives and escalating military repression. This allowed Barrundia and the Liberals to restore reforms that had been sacrificed to appease Carrera.

Meanwhile, the United Provinces of Central America had almost ceased to exist. Nicaragua seceded on 30 April 1838. A month later the federal Congress in San Salvador formally allowed the states to go their separate ways and on 7 July it declared the states to be "sovereign, free, and independent political bodies." Morazán decided it was time to return to San Salvador and restore some semblance of federal control. He believed, incorrectly, that he had greatly weakened the Carrera revolt in Guatemala. He would be no more successful in the other states. Honduras and Costa Rica followed Nicaragua out of the federation before year's end.

Within a month of Morazán's departure, the Conservatives, supported by popular demonstrations in the capital calling for action to prevent a new invasion by Carrera, had regained control of the government. On 22 July 1838 Valenzuela turned over executive power to Rivera Paz. Three days later the legislature decreed a general amnesty for all political acts since 1821, welcomed back exiles, and declared all civil liberties restored. There followed a stream of legislation dismantling the Liberal program and restoring institutions of the colonial period. The legislature provided for State support of the Church, formally declared national sovereignty, reduced the head tax by half, repealed civil marriage and divorce, revoked Gálvez's municipal organization system, and in essence reversed the direction of Guatemala's government.

Despite Conservative control of the government, there were still high-ranking Liberal officers in the Army, which continued its campaign against Carrera's guerrillas. Carrera took Antigua in early September 1838, but Liberal General Carlos Salazar then dealt him a serious defeat at Villa Nueva. Carrera himself escaped into the hills and soon resumed the resistance, but the battle encouraged the Liberals. Morazán returned to Guatemala and in January 1839 he deposed Rivera Paz, replacing him with General Salazar.

Carrera now allied himself with Conservatives in Honduras and Nicaragua, and they joined forces against the Liberals in El Salvador, forcing Morazán's return to that front. Morazán's term as President of the Federation expired on 1 February 1839, and his opponents now claimed that he was the true rebel, for he was in office illegally after that date. Morazán's technical resignation in favor of Vice President Diego Vijil impressed virtually no one. No election had been held, and the federation had all but ceased to exist.

On 13 April 1839 Carrera entered Guatemala City unopposed at the head of a large and orderly army. He promptly restored Rivera Paz as chief of state. He spent the remainder of the year mopping up Liberal resistance in Guatemala and supporting Conservative forces in El Salvador and Honduras. In January

1840 he moved swiftly into Los Altos and crushed the Liberal stronghold at Quetzaltenango. He assured its inhabitants of his continued protection now that he had put Los Altos back on the "road to progress." He promised lower taxes and immediately abolished the head tax. In fact, however, residents of Los Altos would learn that under Carrera the country would be largely run for the benefit of the economic interests of the capital and the central region of the state. The elite of the capital would jealousy guard and narrowly define national development according to their own interests, just as they had in the colonial period. Thus Quetzaltenango would remain distrustful of Carrera and the heart of later revolt against the Conservatives.

A showdown between Morazán and Carrera remained inevitable. Morazán refused to abandoned the federation idea, even though with the fall of Los Altos he held only El Salvador. In March 1840 he invaded Guatemala, outmaneuvering Carrera's forces in the field and entering the capital city on 18 March. On the following day, however, Carrera's troops stormed into the city, completely routing the Liberal Army. Morazán and a few of his officers escaped by sea to Panama. Two years later he returned to Central America for the last time. He briefly usurped power from the moderate Conservatives who had established themselves in Costa Rica under Braulio Carrillo, but another popular uprising cut short his aspirations of reunification, and Morazán died before a firing squad in San José on 15 September 1842.

5

The Republic of Guatemala

Rafael Carrera

Rafael Carrera's decisive defeat of Francisco Morazán in 1840 realigned the balance of power throughout the isthmus. Carrera had already formed an alliance with the Honduran Conservative leader, Francisco Ferrera. Now he dictated terms to the defeated Salvadorans and imposed one of his own lieutenants, Francisco Malespín, as ruler of El Salvador until 1846. In Guatemala, from 1840 to 1844 Carrera held the military power but not the presidency. Carrera skillfully played Liberals off against Conservatives as both vied for control of the government. While the Central American states sometimes declared a desire for reunification, in fact they increased their individual sovereignty.

With Conservatives gaining power in all five states perhaps Carrera might have followed up his victory over Morazán by uniting the isthmus under his own leadership. Yet the Federation idea had become too closely associated with Morazán and the Liberals for the Conservatives to embrace it easily. Strong provincial loyalties in each state, each with its respective caudillo, had developed along with fear and suspicion of Guatemala. Moreover, Carrera had no ambition to reunify the isthmus. Content to dominate the neighboring states, he permitted Costa Rica and Nicaragua to go their own ways. Indeed, even with Conservative leadership it is doubtful that those two states would have again accepted the political hegemony of Guatemala without bitter resistance. In 1842 all of the states except Costa Rica joined in a defensive alliance dedicated to maintaining state sovereignty and preventing restoration of the 1824 Federal Constitution. Although Costa Rica remained aloof from the alliance, her government formally denounced Morazán and the Liberal program in the same year.

In Guatemala the Conservative soon found it difficult to control Carrera. The 1840s were years of political adjustment to caudillismo. Carrera's enormous ego grew with his age, and he demanded obedience and adulation from all. He once referred to a portrait of Napoleon Bonaparte as "Another me!" Carrera's will was law, and his insistence from time to time on the priority of peasant interests sometimes made life uncomfortable for the elite with whom he shared power. He was a remarkably astute politician with a capacity for manipulation. He checked Conservative efforts to dominate the government by giving occasional support to the Liberals. Yet his own interests eventually shifted to the more traditional Conservatism of the oligarchy. The growth of his personal estate may have contributed to this. At the beginning, he controlled only his wife's inherited property, but his properties increased with his military successes. By the time he formally became President in 1844 he and his family had amassed considerable wealth. The creole elite paid a price for Carrera's support of the Conservative agenda, however, for under Carrera ladinos also began to play a larger role in Guatemalan politics. The hold of the European elite over government was clearly broken, even if their social dominance had been restored in Guatemala.

The legislature installed in May 1839 dismantled the remains of the Liberal program. Under the direction of Rivera Paz

—in reality under the guns of Carrera—a disciplined state with restored Hispanic institutions emerged. The assembly began by restoring the religious orders and inviting the exiled archbishop to return. It confirmed a slate of appointments acceptable to the Conservatives (including Carrera as Commanding General of the Army), began a process of consolidating the customs service, and put the treasury in order. Municipal elections in July gave the Conservatives control of Guatemala City. In August the legislature reestablished the national mint and the merchant guild, turning over supervision of road and port works to the latter. Later it revived the office of Corregidor (centralizing control over the country), reestablished education under Church auspices, chartered a national bank, and revived the *residencia* investigation carried out at the conclusion of the term of office for all major public officials. The legislators reduced taxes on foodstuffs in another response to popular opinion, but reinstituted the former alcoholic beverages controls. They abolished the head tax altogether, but restored the tithe tax in support of the Church. They decreed a Declaration of the Rights of the State and its Inhabitants, which, although maintaining in print many civil liberties, clearly turned the direction of the state toward authoritarianism. Roman Catholicism once more became the official religion, and the Church regained its special legal privileges and position as a partner of the State.

In 1840 the reaction continued. The Guatemalan government, in an effort to balance the budget in the face of Carrera's continued military expenditures and a sizable debt, slashed the salaries of public and military officials. Restoration of the tobacco monopoly increased government revenues. With Carrera's collaboration, the government sought to end military abuses against local populations. It also tried to develop the economy through promotion of new crops and subsidies and re-established the Economic Society—another colonial institution—to aid such promotions. Carrera himself proposed protective tariffs for local industries and division of lands by municipalities to promote production of cochineal and silk. Meanwhile, the Church regained some of its confiscated property. In restoring the colonial institutions that the Liberals had suppressed, the Conservatives tied the Guatemala economy to a relatively small group of wealthy landowners and merchants and established a major obstacle toward more dynamic national economic growth. The restoration of the University of San Carlos, with Father Juan José Aycinena as rector until 1854, represented well the aristocratic, pro-clerical, and reactionary philosophy that now prevailed.

Continued turmoil between Liberals and Conservatives in the neighboring states kept Carrera occupied during the early 1840s. Rivera Paz presided over the government, but Carrera held the real power and presided over the Council of State. Conservatives held most important posts. There was some economic progress and construction, especially in the city, but there was still widespread poverty and rural banditry continued to plague sections of the the countryside, despite Carrera's frequent forays to suppress it. Yet mutual distrust remained between Carrera and the Conservative elite that ran the government. These well-heeled oligarchs were mortified at having to treat the rough-hewn, uneducated Carrera with respect and deference. Carrera, for his part, had not forgotten that the Conservatives as well as Liberals had sought his defeat before 1839. Tension developed in 1844 when Carrera asked for more military forces and reorganization of the army. The government begrudgingly yielded to these demands, but in the process Carrera cooled toward the Conservatives and turned to the Liberals for support. He snubbed the new Archbishop, Francisco de Paula García Peláez, by failing to attend either the ceremony welcoming him to the city or his consecration on 6 March. Then, when 2,000 peasants massed near the capital, declaring their opposition to the government, Carrera hurried to the capital from his Pacific coast retreat and quickly took charge. He quickly arranged a peace agreement on 11 March that brought major changes to the government and, at least temporarily, brought back considerable Liberal influence. The resulting Convenio de Guadalupe barred clergymen from holding public office and chastised the Constituent Assembly, which after five years had failed to produce the new constitution that it had been charged to write in 1839. Nor had the assembly, the Supreme Court, nor the government met the needs of the people, it said. Making it clear that the insurgents had no intention of challenging Carrera, who was probably behind the whole incident, the document declared that the peace and security of the state was due "solely to our General-in-Chief." It thus dissolved the Constituent Assembly, transferring its authority to the Council of State which would be popularly elected with one individual from each department and be responsible for writing the new constitution. In doing this it emphasized the money that would be saved by not having to pay the Assembly, making it possible for the public treasury to support the Army without the necessity of forced loans or new taxes. It also restored the army's traditional legal privileges (*fuero*). The Convenio de Guadalupe, with its strong statement of popular values and attitudes toward the government, reflected the reality that neither the Conservative nor Liberal factions represented the rural masses. In this case, the military commanders rallied the peasants to defy the Conservative faction with whom they had earlier allied, but the elite nature of both the Liberal and Conservative parties would over and over again alienate them from the masses. Certainly, it would appear that this whole rebellion was engineered by Carrera in order to curtail the clerical party. Reflecting a mix of Conservative and Liberal principles, it established a new balance in the government, with Carrera and the Liberals gaining at the expense of the clergy. Perhaps more important for the long-term history of Guatemala, the Convenio de Guadalupe definitively established the superiority of the military over the legislature, and it also laid the groundwork for Carrera's accession to the presidency.

As civil disturbances continued to afflict the country, along with continued friction with both Honduras and El Salvador, Carrera assumed greater authority. The government first postponed and then abandoned altogether the election for Council of State. Rivera Paz, in consultation with Carrera, simply appointed a new council, which although it included some prominent Conservatives, had a majority of Liberals. When ultraconservatives, who were noticeably absent from the new council, attempted to regain control, Carrera seized full power. The cabinet resigned on 2 December 1844 and Rivera Paz announced his resignation on the 8th, unwilling or unable to form a new cabinet and announcing that the country needed a change in administration. A new Constituent Congress convened on the same day and elected the moderately liberal José Venacio López, a distinguished jurist, as its president. Under his direction the Congress on 11 December chose Carrera to succeed Rivera Paz as President. Carrera took office three days later, promising to obey the law and work for everyone's welfare. In administering the oath of office López compared General Carrera to Bartolomé de las Casas for his devotion to the well-being of the downtrodden indigenous masses.

Once in office, Carrera quickly mended his relations with the clergy, although he sided with the Liberals in preventing the Jesuits from returning to Guatemala in 1845. He also dealt harshly with another attempted Conservative coup in 1845. Yet, as a new Constituent Congress neared completion of a Constitution in mid-1846, Carrera distanced himself from the Liberals, including José Francisco Barrundia, who had been influential in drafting the document. He even took leave of the presidency in August, turning over power temporarily to Vice President General Vicente Cruz, one of his closest supporters, but of somewhat more Liberal persuasion than Carrera. When the Liberal Congress appeared close to ratifying the Constitution in November, Carrera resumed the presidency, dissolved the Congress and convened a new one that promptly rejected the Constitution.

Despite considerable lawlessness and banditry, Guatemala began to gain some degree of stability under Carrera's strong rule. He continued to meddle in the affairs of El Salvador and Honduras, but also came under considerable influence of the British consul, Frederick Chatfield, who tended to favor the Conservatives throughout the isthmus as friendlier to British commercial interests. Chatfield may have been influential on Carrera's decision to declare Guatemala's absolute independence in 1847. On 9 March of that year the Guatemalan government formally notified the other Central American states of this decision, since all efforts to bring about national reunion had failed. A bi-partisan commission to write a new constitution included the strongly Liberal Pedro Molina, the moderate Liberal Alejandro Marure who had served in both Liberal and Conservative governments, and strongly Conservative Gregorio Urruela. Although the Liberals still theoretically championed Central American union, Molina's enthusiastic acceptance of this assignment suggests that the Liberals accepted collaboration with the Conservatives and the decision to separate Guatemala in a rare display of political unity. Carrera proclaimed a formal Declaration of Independence on 21 March. This long document, doubtless written by Marure with suggestions from others, was essentially an historical essay tracing the failure of the federation and the practical difficulties that had stood in the way. It justified establishment of the new republic on these practical considerations, but held out the possibility of eventual reunion, as Article 5 declared that "the absolute independence in which this republic is now constituted shall never be an obstacle to the reunification of Central America."

This act of independence changed nothing but the name of the country, of course, for Guatemala had been conducting itself along an independent course since 1839, and there was no federal government still in existence from which to secede. Yet the unity that the act seemed to produce among Liberals and Conservatives came from the Liberals' control of the government with the Conservatives hoping that this new emphasis on sovereignty would offer a legal basis for reversing the Liberal trend toward restructuring the state's constitutional framework. The Constitutional Commission quickly produced a draft Constitution which it presented in July 1847. It was a conservative document, but Molina supported it, believing that any constitution was better than none. The unity between Conservatives and Liberals now concentrated on forming a coalition that could rid itself of the caudillo and the influence of his barbaric associates, so that the proposed constitution awaited only the convening of a new assembly.

Uncomfortable with the patrician elite and clergy of the capital, Carrera kept them off balance with frequent changes of ministers and with intrigue and collaboration with their political opponents. Liberal participation in his government, however, did not significantly change the Conservative tone of the regime. Playing off Liberals against Conservatives was for a time an effective way for the caudillo to maintain his control, but the continued turmoil and banditry in the countryside had evolved into a new rebellion in eastern Guatemala by 1847 and created doubts about his ability to continue to command the rural masses. Led by one of Carrera's own followers, General Serapio Cruz, brother of Vicente, this rebellion was beginning to resemble that which Carrera himself had led in 1837. The failure of Carrera to satisfy all of the grievances of the montañeses and the agitation of some Liberals allowed this movement to flourish. With Carrera in the field, the Liberals in the capital became bolder and began to encourage a freer press. Carrera had managed to postpone elections for the Constituent Assembly to ratify the new Constitution, but in the face of spreading rebellion he finally yielded to demands for the election in June 1848. Liberal victory in this election created a new crisis. The government tried to discredit the new Assembly that convened in August, but Carrera made it clear that he would honor the results and turn over his authority to the new Assembly. This decision may have been more due to the unfavorable military situation that was developing, for despite Carrera's victories in several key battles, the rebels were extending the territory under their control.

When the new Assembly convened on 15 August 1848, presided over by the aging Pedro Molina, recently released from prison, Carrera sent it his resignation and went into exile in Chiapas. The Assembly quickly chose Lic. Juan Antonio Martínez, a Liberal merchant, as provisional president. This was a serious slight to Vice President Vicente Cruz, who now joined the rebels with his brother, Serapio. Unable to quell the rural rebellion or even to cope with the Guatemala City Council, which remained in Conservative hands, Martínez resigned in November. His successor, José Bernardo Escobar, tried to form a unity government that included Conservatives as well as Liberals, but was unable to negotiate a settlement with the Cruz brothers. He, too, resigned before the end of 1848.

Under strong pressure from the Guatemala City elite and facing possible invasion of the city by montañés guerrillas, the Assembly now turned to a military man to save them. Colonel Mariano Paredes had enjoyed some success in campaigning against the rebels. Largely apolitical, he had served under both Mariano Gálvez and Rafael Carrera. Paredes took charge with a vigor not seen in his two predecessors. Although he had to appoint some Liberals to his government to maintain a satisfactory relationship with the Assembly, Paredes astutely recognized that the Liberals had lost whatever advantage they had held earlier and he organized his government largely along Conservative lines. Paredes was privately much influenced by Luis Batres, Carrera's Conservative Prime Minister before his overthrow in 1848. Paredes took over full command of the army on 18 January 1849 from Liberal Field Marshall Francisco Cáscara, who had resigned when Paredes became President. Paredes imposed a forced loan on property holders to finance his military buildup and then quickly reached a preliminary agreement with Serapio Cruz to end the civil war.

Fear that Carrera would return hung over the Liberals throughout their tenure. He remained dangerously close in Comitán, Chiapas, and maintained communication with his Conservative allies in Guatemala. He sold many of his assets in Guatemala before the government could confiscate them and he now used receipts from those sales to build up a military force. On 24 January Carrera wrote to Paredes, announcing that he was returning to Guatemala to restore peace and order. He asked the government to grant him amnesty and apologize for the indignities he had suffered.

In response, Paredes reconvened the Assembly, which quickly accepted the peace agreement with Cruz. This provided for General Vicente Cerna to become commander-in-chief of the armed forces, essentially returning control of the country to the Army. On 9 February 1849 the rebel Army of the People, with the Cruz brothers riding at its head, marched into Guatemala and joined the regular army under Cerna's command. Paredes then pursued policies that minimized the differences between Liberals and Conservatives and united the country under strong military rule.

Although the Cruz brothers and their forces were now loyal to the government, other guerrilla bands continued the insurgency in the East. Vicente Cruz died in a skirmish with guerrillas in Jalapa. Meanwhile there were rumors of a new Los Altos secession from Guatemala and of the impending invasion of the western highlands by General Carrera. His Army of Restoration, raiding around Huehuetenango in the West, was gaining support among Indian villages there. Although Paredes responded to these threats with military repression, he also appointed a commission to negotiate with Carrera. Their instructions were to "promote an arrangement respecting the person of this chief, to reestablish peace and tranquility in the pueblos that his forces have occupied." The influence of Luis Batres was undoubtedly important, as was the grim news of the Caste War in Yucatan (1847–1855), fueling fears of a general indigenous uprising in Guatemala. A critical factor here was news that the popular and dashing Corregidor of Suchitepéquez, General José Víctor Zavala, had defected to Carrera, allowing him to take control of Quetzaltenango.

Over the bitter opposition of Molina and Barrundia, who argued for a death penalty against Carrera, Paredes cracked down hard on the press and proceeded to negotiate an agreement that rescinded the earlier prohibition of Carrera's return to Guatemala, re-commissioned him as a lieutenant general in the Army, and agreed to pay all the expenses of his forces. Carrera in turn agreed to respect the orders of the Paredes government. This accord quickly brought peace to Los Altos, but trouble continued in the East which Paredes argued was a further justification for reinstating Carrera. After consolidating his position in Quetzaltenango, Carrera marched into Guatemala City on 7 August 1849. The Conservatives were clearly in control now and the 1848 Revolution was over. He assumed command of the Guatemalan Army the next day and launched a campaign to end the uprising in the eastern montaña. He blamed the revolt on the Liberals for the same reasons as in 1837. He called on all, but especially the clergy, for help in this struggle. This occupied Carrera for the rest of 1849 and throughout 1850, but he also consolidated his control of the country by forcing the removal of Liberals from political offices and solidifying his solid alliance with the Conservatives. Gradually, Carrera reduced the threat from the East, but the uprising did not completely die down for a long time, as the rebels often fled across the borders into Honduras and El Salvador.

The Revolution of 1848 reflected two important social movements in Guatemalan history. On the one hand, it was a final effort by the Liberals who had arisen with national independence to control the government and direct it under policies put forward by Morazán and Gálvez. They temporarily brought down the dictatorship of Rafael Carrera, but to do this they had allied themselves with the other social movement—the restless peasantry of the montaña and other regions of the country—that had smoldered and flamed up ever since 1837. While these two movements had some common foes, they were nevertheless largely incompatible, for the rural people remained staunchly Conservative and distrustful of Liberal land policy. Moreover, the Liberals were still led by members of prominent Guatemala City families who failed to appreciate fully the importance of regional leaders to their cause. While the 1848 revolution reflected the important Liberal force coming out of Los Altos, the Liberals in power in 1848 were not able to consolidate their victory or to incorporate the various rebel military groups operating in the country to the extent necessary to establish a government that could govern against the combined strength of the conservative Guatemala City elite and the caudillo Carrera. Thus, it was not surprising that Carrera could reorganize his forces and return to Guatemala, this time to establish a strongly Conservative dictatorship that would endure for two more decades.

Carrera's consolidation of Conservative strength in Guatemala threatened Liberal gains not only in Guatemala but also in El Salvador, Honduras, and Nicaragua. The establishment in 1849 of the moderately Conservative government of Juan Rafael Mora in Costa Rica, however, laid the foundation for a Guatemalan-Costa Rica axis that, with British encouragement, eventually helped to bring a measure of unity to the whole region under Conservative leadership. Carrera and the Conservatives opposed Liberal efforts to reunite the three middle republics. Military encounters between the two sides culminated in 1851 when a new unionist government formed at Chinandega, Nicaragua, launched an invasion of Guatemala. Carrera stopped this maneuver at San José la Arada, south of Chiquimula, on 2 February 1851, in the greatest military victory of his career. He followed it up with an offensive into El Salvador that brought down the Salvadoran government and replaced it with one more acceptable to Carrera. Carrera and his victorious Army returned to Guatemala City on 3 March to a triumphant celebration, capped with promotion of Carrera to the rank of Captain General with an annual salary of 4,000 pesos. Arada brought Carrera enormous prestige and power and assured his return to the presidency of Guatemala. Arada was a death blow to the efforts of Barrundia and the middle-state Liberals to reorganize the federation. The Liberal-Conservative rivalry continued to plague those states, a prelude to the takeover of Nicaragua by the North American adventurer William Walker in the mid-1850s.

By the end of 1851 Carrera's position within the Guatemalan power structure had been thoroughly established. Praised and honored by President Paredes for his defense of Guatemala, Carrera skillfully orchestrated a new Conservative Party that combined Carrera and his military chiefs with Church leaders, leading merchants, and the established families headed by the Aycinenas, Piñols, and Pavóns. It was a powerful consolidation of the social and economic power of the country, against which the Liberal "upstarts" could muster little defense, especially when the Conservatives could count on widespread popular support as well.

A stifling dictatorship settled over the country. Carrera was one of the classic Conservative caudillos in mid-nineteenth century Latin America and he ruled with an iron fist. The regime had the same distrust of non-Spanish foreigners that had characterized colonial times. The return to the Hispanic heritage stopped short of actually returning the country to Spanish rule, as did happen briefly in the Dominican Republic, but in 1851 Carrera restored the Spanish red and gold to the Guatemalan national flag, where those colors remained symbolically for twenty years.

Threatening the Liberals with death in popular slogans, Carrera made it clear that their residence in Guatemala depended on their cooperation with him. No longer were there the occasional alliances with Liberals that had occurred during the first decade of his domination. Carrera was unforgiving as he proceeded to establish his absolute rule. A Conservative Assembly decreed a Constitution in October 1851 that provided for an authoritarian government, which it then elected Carrera to head. Although his term of office officially began on 1 January 1852, he was installed ahead of schedule on 6 November 1851 for a four-year term. Three years later a General Council of Authorities extended his term to life. His dictatorship was total from then until his death in 1865. From his death bed he named Field Marshal Vicente Cerna as his successor. Under Cerna the Conservative regime survived for six more years.

The Conservatives' attitude toward the indigenous population reflected the reactionary philosophy of looking back to the Spanish era. An 1839 Indian Code recognized the importance of protecting "this numerous class," and improving " its customs and civilization." Replacing the Liberal program that the Conservatives said mistreated and exploited the Indians under the pretext of equal treatment for all, the new code restored the colonial system that "compelled them to work, to provide public service on certain projects, and to pay taxes... but also gave them protection against the influential and the powerful in their land claims." This new code reversed Gálvez's idea of incorporating the Indian into Western civilization. Instead, it called for reestablishment of the office of Indian interpreter and ordered local officials to translate decrees into indigenous languages. The Conservatives thus replaced Gálvez's exploitive policy of assimilation with a paternalistic approach that insured survival of a large segment of the Guatemalan population as a separate Indian nation, segregated from the mainstream of national life, a situation that continued in parts of Guatemala even into the present century.

The Conservatives thus discarded the idealism of the Liberals for a romanticism that glorified a brighter past and emphasized their common Spanish-Catholic heritage. Defending the regime in the pages of the government's *Gaceta de Guatemala*, one of Guatemala's most noted writers, José Milla, on 9 December 1849 editorialized persuasively that Guatemala had to develop institutions that conformed to its own customs. What was right for the United States or Great Britain, he suggested, was probably not right for Russia, and the adoption of liberal institutions in Central America had brought disastrous consequences and retarded its development. The Liberals, he chided, can "talk about the glorious system, the order, the liberty... [and] draw the happiest picture, not of what is, but of what should be; but who will have been deceived? Will thinking people who see and know the foundation of things, those that attend to business within the framework of reality? Doubtless not."

The Catholic clergy recovered its old position and privileges. The government revived some old taxes, but kept its expenses at modest levels. It left most development to the private sector, but under government supervision. Insofar as powerful foreign interests—notably the British—would permit, it abandoned free trade. Guatemalan exports expanded modestly, establishing a favorable trade balance that helped reduce the debt. Where the Liberals had been eager to adopt foreign innovation, the trend now turned anti-foreign and nationalistic. Foreigners continued to play the dominant role in overseas trade, but now Spanish as well as British merchants received favors. Culturally, the period was one of stagnation, but Conservative rule nevertheless achieved greater economic growth than had been made in the early years after independence, even though it was less than the more advanced nations of the Western world experienced in the mid-nineteenth century. Yet most economic activity remained at the subsistence level and exports represented only a tiny part of the total economy. The xenophobic tone of the Carrera years imposed a certain isolation on the country. While Carrera retained veto power, he allowed the Conservative elite to run the country. His concern for the poor may have waned as his own riches increased, but there can be little doubt that, through charity and paternalism, his government provided a better life for the masses than had the progressivism of the Gálvez Liberals, even if it was no improvement over the colonial period.

Although suspicious of foreign colonization schemes, the government nevertheless continued to entertain such projects. But, significantly, Guatemala turned from the Protestant English to a company of Belgian Catholics for development of its north coast. This Belgian colony at Santo Tomás de Castilla hardly had more success in the 1840s than had the English in the previous decade at Abbotsville, on the Rio Polochic, but these projects did result in improved shipping service. The English company's steamer, the *Verapaz*, linked the Golfo Dulce with Belize, thereby increasing the commercial dependence of Guatemala on that port. The Belgian company later provided service with Belgium on an irregular basis. By 1850 regular, if sometimes unreliable, steamship service connected the Caribbean coast with Europe and North America.

If the Conservatives imposed a certain isolation on Guatemala, the industrial revolution inevitably still affected the country. External forces thus had as much to do with Guatemalan development in the nineteenth century as did internal turmoil. The growth of production and commerce moved the country closer to dependency on the industrial world. Major improvements in transportation encouraged this growth and led to a notable shift of commerce from the Caribbean to Pacific Coast ports. The British dominated the trade of early independent Guatemala. The British presence there took several forms. In some instances it was the intentional manifestation of imperial policy.

In others, however, it reflected the overzealousness of local British diplomats, notably Frederick Chatfield, who at times exceeded rather considerably his instructions and authority. Still other actions came from private British subjects residing in the area and acting with no authority from the British government. These distinctions also characterized U.S. activities, which as the century progressed began to rival those of Great Britain. British log cutters and smugglers had established a strong British foothold at Belize. If their principal activity was commercial, territorial expansion was not absent from British policy. After independence British sovereignty over the eastern coast of Central America came closer to reality.

Belize's population grew notably, especially when slaves convicted of insurrection in Barbados were brought in, but there was little work for slaves in the colony, which had fewer than 300 white residents in the 1820s. All efforts to turn it into an agricultural colony failed and it remained mainly an entrepôt for British-Guatemalan trade. The slavery question troubled relations between Belize and Guatemala, where slavery had declined notably in the late colonial period and had been abolished altogether after independence. But fugitive slaves from Belize sought refuge in the Petén. It was difficult for either federal or Guatemalan authorities to enforce their wishes in that remote region, but irritation arose when Belizeans pursued fugitive slaves into the Petén. British pretensions in the region challenged the new republic's sovereignty and promoted nationalist sentiments that had little to do with the fugitive slave issue itself. Despite the close trade relations developing between Britain and Guatemala, Liberal disillusionment with Great Britain began. By the time the Conservatives came to power, Britain herself had abolished slavery.

British merchants did not generally establish themselves in Guatemala as they did in several Latin American states that had major ports on the coast, but there were a few notable exceptions. Of these the most important was the Belize firm of Marshal Bennett, which established the Guatemalan firm of William Hall and Carlos Meany in the 1820s. In the same decade George Skinner and Charles Klée established mercantile families that continue to be important in Guatemala to the present day.

From 1825 forward, Britain steadily reduced her duties on nearly all Central American export produce. Cochineal and indigo (mostly from El Salvador) became Guatemala's principal items of foreign exchange as the British textile industry expanded the market for these dyes. Cochineal, produced from a small insect that thrived on the nopal cactus, became Guatemala's principal export in the mid-nineteenth century. The regions around Amatitlán and Antigua were the principal areas of nopal cultivation for this purpose, but as exports grew after 1840 it expanded into other areas as well. In 1856 the discovery of coal-tar aniline dyes threatened the natural dye industry and eventually led to the ruin of the cochineal trade. Income from expanded cotton exports enabled some Guatemalan planters to make an easier transition from cochineal to coffee production, which took several years to develop. The Civil War in the United States (1861–1865) allowed Guatemala temporarily to gain a larger share of the international cotton market, accounting for 19 percent of Guatemalan exports by 1865, but it dropped off sharply thereafter. Cochineal dropped from more than 90 percent of Guatemalan exports in the 1840s to only about 33 percent by 1871. Meanwhile, the Conservative government encouraged coffee cultivation in the 1850s, so that it had reached 50 percent of Guatemalan exports by 1871.

Britain also accounted for more than half of Guatemala's imports in the mid-nineteenth century and British loans and bond issues furthered British domination of Guatemala's international trade. The fiasco of the Barclay, Herring, & Richardson loan of 1825 certainly dampened investor interest in Central America, but loans from British firms to Guatemala nevertheless continued. The Liberal governments of the 1820s encouraged such arrangements, and although Conservative governments were more wary, such transactions did not end altogether. The Carrera government, in negotiating a loan with the London firm of Isaac & Samuel in 1856 to pay off its earlier debts, for instance, had to pledge 50 percent of its customs receipts to debt service. Such arrangements involved British nationals in the internal finance of the government to the extent of compromising its national sovereignty. Guatemala also made concessions to English mining companies, but, undercapitalized and lacking adequate transportation infrastructure, they failed to increase significantly mineral production during the early national period.

Other foreigners also played important roles in Guatemala. A smattering of Frenchmen, Italians, Germans, and Belgians joined the few English residents. Several European military officers served in the Army. The new Republic of Guatemala quickly signed commercial treaties with most of the major European nations before 1850. Spain refused to recognize Guatemalan independence until 1863, but she was quicker to ensure continuance of Spanish commerce with her former colony. Even as she encouraged pro-Spanish insurgencies following Central American independence, Spain continued to permit Guatemalan trade with Cuban and Spanish ports. The United States, although destined eventually to play a massive role on the isthmus, had little contact with the region before 1850. A few diplomats and travelers—most notably, John Lloyd Stephens[1]—recorded their impressions, and this developed some North American interest in the isthmus, but trade remained a minor consideration until later in the century. The United States was prompt to recognize the independence of Central America, but made no overt effort to

[1] See his wonderful *Incidents of Travel in Central America, Chiapas and Yucatan*, 2 vols. (New York: Harper & Brothers, 1841), with many more recent editions and printings.

check British expansion until after the war with Mexico (1846–1848).

In addition to the continued differences between Liberals and Conservatives that manifested themselves in both internal civil wars and wars among the Central American states, problems with neighboring Mexico also led to some difficulties for Guatemala. Mexico attempted to expand the frontiers of Chiapas into Soconusco. Carrera, cultivating friendly relations with Mexico's President Antonio López de Santa Anna, whom he admired, successfully resisted the Mexicans, although the issue was to come up again after his death. Further tension in the border regions resulted from the Caste War. Yucatán, never reconciled to Mexican rule, actually seceded in 1838, and the peninsula remained unstable even after its reincorporation into the Mexican republic in 1845. The bloody revolt of the Santa Cruz Maya, who were nearly successful in driving their white and ladino masters from Yucatán, caused widespread disruption in southern Yucatán and created apprehension in Guatemala. Many Yucatecans fled into Belize and Guatemala, causing a crisis of law and order in the former, although in the long run, providing badly needed population to develop the economy there.

The most serious threat to Central America sovereignty in the nineteenth century was the takeover of Nicaragua by the filibuster William Walker. Walker came to Nicaragua in support of Liberals there and Conservatives in all five states joined forces to defeat him in a campaign that Central Americans referred to as the "National War." Although offered command of this Central American army, Carrera chose not to go to Nicaragua himself, but he sent more troops than any other state and Guatemalan officers and troops were crucial to bringing about Walker's surrender in 1857. Returning troops, however, brought a new cholera epidemic to the country, with Carrera's wife, Doña Petrona, being among its victims in 1857.

The "National War" discredited the United States in Central America. The interest the United States had shown in the 1850s waned rapidly as they became embroiled in their own bloodbath of the 1860s. Guatemala was cool toward an effort made by President Lincoln to settle former slaves in Central America, although some ex-slaves, as well as Confederate landowners, did settle in Belize. After the Civil War, concern with southern Reconstruction and western settlement occupied U.S. energies and capital. Yankee capital had been important in building the Panama Railway completed in 1855. This had caused a rapid shift in commerce from the Caribbean to the more accessible Pacific Coast, nearer the centers of population and production and with less lowland jungle and marshland to traverse. Guatemala benefitted greatly from the shift of trade to the Pacific Coast. Freight costs dropped rapidly. Cart roads connected the producing regions to the Pacific ports, especially Puerto San José, and beginnings were made on railroads. Regular steamship service connected these ports with the Panama Railway and opened the Atlantic to them. The shift in Guatemala from Caribbean to Pacific ports was dramatic. Imports via Caribbean ports dropped from a value of more than four million dollars between 1853–1858 to less than two million between 1859–1864, while imports through Pacific ports rose during the same periods from about 2 million to 5.5 million. The Caribbean coast, now neglected, sank into a gloomy despair. At Belize, the entrepôt for the region since independence, the volume of trade dropped by more than half between 1854 and 1856 and continued to decline thereafter.

This decline of Belize prompted British efforts to revitalize that port. In the Wyke-Aycinena Treaty of 1859 Guatemala agreed to recognize British sovereignty over Belize in return for a British promise to construct a road from the Caribbean to the Guatemalan capital. The British then made Belize a Crown Colony (British Honduras) in 1862. Hoping to turn the road into a means of restoring Belize's lost commercial glory, the British began surveys, but costs, difficulties, and higher priorities delayed the project. The treaty had not specified the precise route of the proposed road, but the Guatemalans intended for it to terminate at their own Caribbean port, Santo Tomás. The British, however, intended to lay the road directly to Belize. This issue never being resolved, the Guatemalans finally abrogated the treaty and proceeded to construct a railroad on their own to the Caribbean, leaving the Belize questions smoldering almost to the present.

Conservative rule of Guatemala in the mid-nineteenth century brought some much-needed stability to the new republic and definitively ended the Central American Federation. Rafael Carrera was one of Latin America's classic nineteenth-century caudillos, as he restored Guatemala's Spanish heritage and protected its indigenous population. As such he was responsible for preserving much that was unique about the country. Conservative hegemony would not last long beyond his death in 1865, and Liberal resurgence thereafter would challenge both the Spanish heritage and indigenous autonomy, while seeking to accelerate the pace of economic growth.

6

Liberal Guatemala

Justo Rufino Barrios

The decline of cochineal caused some economic dislocation to Guatemala by the 1860s. Yet Guatemala's porous volcanic soil, the constant year-round temperature, and a single rainy season made its highlands ideally suited for coffee production. Following the lead of Costa Rica, Guatemala began to produce significant amounts of coffee during the Conservative years, but it was under subsequent Liberal regimes that coffee exports propelled the modernization and economic growth that the Liberal rhetoric had promised. By 1855 coffee *fincas* were springing up around Cobán, Antigua, and Amatitlán, and coffee replaced cochineal in the latter two areas. From there, coffee spread to the western highlands and Pacific coastal slopes. The value of coffee among all Guatemala exports rose from one percent in 1860 to 44 percent in 1870, when it became the largest single export commodity, a position it has held ever since. The high quality of Guatemalan coffee placed it among the highest priced in the world.

The transfer of power from Conservatives to Liberals in the latter third of the nineteenth-century accelerated the trend toward modernization, with increased dependence on coffee and other exports. The late-nineteenth century Liberals, although they shared the utilitarian idealism of earlier Liberals, were more impressed with the tenets of positivist materialism. More cynical than their forebears, they believed themselves to be more practical leaders. Certainly, economic progress concerned them more than establishment of a political utopia. Dictatorship continued to characterize Guatemalan government, but with important differences from Carrera's long rule.

Carrera's unprogressive government inevitably dissatisfied younger and ambitious Guatemalans. During the 1860s a core of positivist-oriented intellectuals at the University of San Carlos laid the groundwork for a new generation of Liberal leaders. The series of revolts that transferred power from Conservatives to Liberals in Central America began in El Salvador, where Gerardo Barrios came to power after leading Salvadoran troops in the National War against William Walker. In 1858, as head of the provisional government of El Salvador, Barrios announced liberal educational, political, and economic reforms and then defiantly ordered the remains of Francisco Morazán brought from Costa Rica to San Salvador, where they were reburied with state honors. While assuring the Salvadoran president of his continued friendship, Carrera assembled an army near the Salvadoran border. When Barrios began to restrict the clergy's traditional power in 1863, Carrera invaded. Barrios soundly defeated Carrera's force at Cojutepeque, but failed to follow up his victory. This allowed Carrera to regroup and launch a new offensive that before the year ended toppled Barrios and replaced him as president with a Conservative, Francisco Dueñas.

The death of Carrera in 1865, however, signaled Liberal revolts in Guatemala. Carrera's chosen successor, General Vicente Cerna, put down these uprisings, while at the same time moderating the reactionary tone of the government. In Honduras, however, Liberals established a shaky government that allowed Guatemalan exiles a safe haven there. In April 1871 these Guatemalans joined with Honduran forces to defeat Dueñas in El Salvador and install the Liberal Field Marshal Santiago González, who resumed the reformist and anticlerical policies of Barrios. Salvadoran refusal to indemnify Honduras for her aid in ousting the Conservatives led to a long, sordid history of irresponsible meddling in each other's internal affairs. Such activities became all too common in nineteenth-century Central America and served as a background for the joint United States-Mexican attempts to bring stability there during the first decade of the twentieth century.

Meanwhile, in Guatemala, Miguel García Granados, Serapio Cruz, and Justo Rufino Barrios, with aid from the Liberal Mexican President Benito Juárez, led the Liberal revolt against Cerna. Cruz died in battle in 1870, but Barrios and García Granados defeated Cerna in June 1871. García Granados, a member of one of Guatemala's leading families, had long been a lone Liberal voice in the Guatemalan legislature. Barrios had been important in planting coffee in the departments of Los Altos and represented the long repressed Liberal elite in that region. He had participated in plots against Cerna since 1867. In 1873, after the brief administration of the well-meaning but less aggressive García Granados, Barrios took over the government and established the style of Guatemalan dictators for nearly a century. Developing a professional military as his political base, he ruled with firmness and intolerance for dissent. He established his Liberal University of San Carlos classmate, Marcos Aurelio Soto, as President of Honduras in 1876 and supported a series of Liberals in El Salvador. Ambitions of realizing Morazán's dream of a united Central American federation, however, brought him into conflict with his neighbors and resulted in his defeat and death on the battlefield at Chalchuapa, El Salvador, on 2 April 1885.

The Liberal Reforma created new elites and permitted the rise of new middle sectors that would inevitably play larger roles in Guatemala's economy, society, and government. The rapid advances made by the United States and Western Europe in the nineteenth century impressed the Liberals. The scientific emphasis of the "sociocracy" called for by Auguste Comte and other French positivists and the application of Darwinian evolutionary theory to society as proclaimed by Herbert Spencer appealed to this new group of political and intellectual leaders. The new Liberals were less idealistic than their predecessors of the Morazán days. While they did not formally abandon democratic promises, they now believed that economic growth was needed before political democracy could work. Viewing themselves as scientific realists, their priorities were now order and progress. At the same time, personal and family allegiances still held a dominant place in the political and social structure, obscuring the importance of ideology at times. During the half-century that followed clear patterns emerged that reflected their focus on material development, their anticlericalism, their faith in scientific and technical education, their rejection of the metaphysical, their willingness to postpone political democracy through what Comte called "republican dictatorships," their emulation and imitation of northern European and North American values, and their insensitivity to the needs of the working-class (perhaps, understandable, given the political support those classes had provided to the Conservative caudillos).

With legislation friendly to foreign capital, the government encouraged export crops. Coffee production, already important as a replacement for cochineal, received the most attention in the late nineteenth century. Favored by subsidies, tax exemptions, and the promise of large profits, planters cultivated new lands. Foreigners played an important role in this expansion, although production remained in large part in Guatemalan hands. When foreigners did enter coffee production, they were usually immigrant settlers who remained in the country and became a part of the local society, unlike those later involved in the exploitation of bananas. Germans, especially in the Verapaz, produced an extraordinarily large percentage of Guatemala's coffee. Production soared in the 1880s and coffee has continued as the principal export ever since. World demand for coffee rose rapidly in that decade, and while production more than doubled, prices tripled, producing vast increases in profits. The Germans led the way in technology and processing of the coffee, and, most important, through their contacts and the assistance of their consuls they tapped new markets in Europe and North America. German merchants often financed much of the rapid expansion by extending credits to their nationals in the producing areas. United States coffee importers were more reluctant to agree to such arrangements, but by 1913 they had also become major purchasers of Guatemala coffee. By then, coffee accounted for more than 85 percent of Guatemala's exports.

Mindful of the dangers of monoculture, the government encouraged diversification. Sugar, bananas, cotton, chicle, cacao, rubber, timber, and sarsaparilla joined coffee among Guatemala's exports. The government provided land free or on easy terms for those who developed new crops. Some commodities, such as livestock, wheat, fruits, and vegetables became more important for local consumption than for export, but still contributed to economic growth.

The government launched roads, railroads, and new deepwater ports on both coasts. The obstacles were great and the costs very high, but these works were the most important achievements of the era. A Ministry of Development (*Fomento*), established to promote all aspects of the economy, supervised these infrastructure projects, although much that was accomplished came through private enterprise. Foreign and internal loans provided capital for the projects, but they rarely brought the returns expected and thus contributed to the deepening public debt. Corruption also drained away both energy and funds, as dictators built roads to favor their own special interests at the expense of national development. Despite the Liberals' attacks on class privilege, more often than not they simply replaced an older privileged elite with a new group. Critics of Justo Rufino Barrios accused him of doing this when he promoted the interests of the formerly-neglected western departments of Guatemala (Los Altos).

Railroad construction was painfully slow. Concessions to foreign companies failed to raise sufficient capital to complete the projects. Torrential rains, steep terrain, and dense vegetation created problems that were virtually unknown to the engineers who had built the railroads of North America and Europe. Before 1900 a railway had been completed from the capital to the Pacific port, but almost nothing had been done to connect the capital and the producing areas with the more distant Caribbean coast. The same was true with highways. A good highway on the Pacific side connected Guatemala City with Puerto San José, but there was little progress on the road toward the Atlantic. Stagecoach lines preceded the railways. Forced labor provided much of the manpower for road construction. The law required every male to contribute four days or two pesos annually toward road works.

The newly-opened port of Champerico, on the Pacific, served Quetzaltenango and Los Altos. On the Caribbean, the government first revived the interest in Livingston that had begun during the Gálvez administration, but then turned to Puerto Barrios. Communications improved, though more slowly than in most of the rest of the world, as telegraph lines sprang up along the principal routes. A marine cable completed in 1880 provided direct communication with major cities of the world. Telephone service began in government offices in Guatemala and Quetzaltenango in 1884, and soon thereafter there were phones in the other major towns, although both quality and quantity of service left much to be desired.

The positivists believed that expanded productivity and exports would spark an industrial revolution that would lead Guatemala into the same sort of sophisticated economies enjoyed by Western Europe and the United States. With the greater revenue from exports, they expected the general standard of living to rise and secondary industries to spring up to satisfy the needs of the people. In fact, little of this sort of chain reaction took place. Although the government ostensibly encouraged manufacturing, the economic growth was insufficient to stimulate adequate domestic markets, nor was their technology, skilled labor, or capital in sufficient quantity. To be sure, a few textile mills opened, along with some other shops and small factories, but it was hardly an "industrial revolution." Between 1870 and 1900 Guatemala's volume of trade increased by more than 20 times. Instead of contributing to industrial development within Guatemala, however, the export profits were simply spent on imported goods or invested abroad. The increase in consumption was uneven, as most of the population remained at the subsistence level. Imports rose greatly, paid for with the exchange gained in exports, but Guatemala maintained a favorable balance of trade throughout the period.

The number of foreign commercial firms operating in Guatemala soared. Because of the shortage of currency and financial institutions, some of them also became financial agents, carrying on a brisk banking business. Their commercial paper often served as negotiable currency and facilitated credit operations. Banks proliferated, both foreign and domestic. A national bank served as the vehicle for government financing of public works projects, either through direct loans or through the sale of bonds to domestic and foreign investors. Tariffs accounted for more than half of total government income, which rose with the increasing trade and rising import duties. Government officials believed that future increases would be even larger. The Liberals staunchly opposed direct taxes on income or property. Other sources of income for the government were state monopolies, such as liquor and tobacco; sales taxes; other taxes and licenses; and charges for services, such as the telegraph, post office, or the mint. Despite increased revenues, unfortunately, corruption, poor organization, faulty fiscal systems, and poorly trained personnel seriously hindered government efficiency.

Notwithstanding the failure to industrialize or to develop a more diversified economy, the country advanced notably during the late nineteenth and early twentieth centuries. After years of warfare and economic stagnation, there was rapid population growth. Medical advances cut the mortality rate, and opportunities for employment drew rural people into the city. More active government participation in the economy expanded the bureaucracy. Guatemala City and Quetzaltenango took on a more elegant, modern appearance, as public works projects lighted the streets, erected grand public buildings, theaters, and stadiums, and laid out parks, race tracks, monuments, and aqueducts. Street railways—first mule-drawn and later electrified—facilitated greater economic growth and flexibility, as public services in general expanded. The influx of foreigners and travelers stimulated brisk increases in the numbers and quality of hotels and restaurants, which had hardly existed before the Liberal resurgence. In this business, as in others, foreigners dominated, and German, French, English, and Italian names were often seen on the signboards of these hostelries, lending a superficial cosmopolitan air to the capital. Inevitably, increases in vice, prostitution, and crime accompanied the population growth. Provincial towns, on the other hand, declined, intensifying the startling contrast between the capital and the rural areas of the country. The capital became the showplace of the elites who controlled the society and economy.

The urgency of material development seemed to justify strong executive leadership with an inherent lack of faith in popular democracy, contributing to the formation of military dictatorships. A new Constitution (1879) reiterated the republican principles of earlier Liberals, but the institutions that evolved created a centralized, executive-run government with the military as the real arbiter of public affairs. Not surprisingly, military men tended to dominate the presidency for much of modern Guatemalan history. The *personalismo* that had characterized the Carrera regime remained a factor, but now support rested upon a more professional military force rather than upon the rabble or upon personal armies. A salient feature of these dictators was that they appointed military officers, under close presidential regulation, to control local areas. With police power, these *jefes políticos* (replacing the *corregidores* of the earlier period), maintained order and a climate favorable to the foreign and native planters and entrepreneurs who benefitted from the system. The methods of the Liberal dictators were such that some critics have observed that there was little difference between Carrera's Conservatism and Barrios's Liberalism. There were, of course, real differences in the manner in which these dictators ruled, but more important were the institutional changes that accompanied the social revolution of the Liberal era. For the first time, large, permanent bureaucracies developed to carry on national administration. The improved communications and more professional military forces enabled the bureaucracy to rule the rural hinterland to a much greater degree than ever before.

This restructuring of Guatemala's government accommodated a new dominant class. The Liberals now abolished or reduced the importance of traditional Hispanic institutions. The old privileged merchant guild (*consulado*) saw its development functions absorbed by the new Ministry of Development and its judicial privileges incorporated into the ordinary civil and criminal court system. Later, the Economic Society—once regarded as a Liberal institution but now associated with the Conservative elite of the capital—was also suppressed. The Liberals ended other vestiges of Spanish colonial rule. The most important institutions, the Church and the Army, both underwent substantial change. The Church, on which the Conservatives had depended to cement their alliance with the masses, lost its former wealth and position. The government confiscated Church lands and expropriated the endowments of religious orders. They expelled some orders from the country altogether, forbade clerics to wear clerical garb except in discharge of their religious functions, banned or restricted religious processions, permitted civil birth registration, first legalized and then made compulsory civil marriage, established religious toleration and welcomed Protestant immigrants and missionaries, and abolished compulsory tithe taxes and the clerical *fuero*. Once more they ended the Church's monopoly on education and restricted the moral censorship that the Church had been allowed to impose. In addition, other projects of the Church, such as hospitals, charity, and care of orphans and the aged, began to be taken over by the State. Reductions in the number of clergy left many rural areas without priests, thereby diminishing the Church's influence over the peasant population.

The Church fought back. It excommunicated President Barrios and other officials. Barrios and his successors responded by exiling the archbishop and bishops, and in the end the Liberals succeeded in reducing the power and prestige of the Church. While it remained the refuge of Conservative upper class diehards, the Church lost the strong authority it had once held over the masses. Although not totally ended even today, the dominant role the clergy had played in rural areas became minor. This was one of the most important changes ever to take place in Guatemala.

The Guatemalan Army had been Carrera's personal militia, composed of ill-disciplined, poorly-paid rabble who enjoyed privilege and prestige of a sort, but also evoked universal disdain and fear. The Liberal regimes after 1871 turned it into a more professional organization of a permanent, institutional nature. The enlisted troops, it is true, for the most part remained ragged, poorly paid, barefoot, and not very "professional," but the officer corps was institutionalized through a national military academy, the Escuela Politécnica, established in 1873. The Liberals hired foreign officers as instructors, and a few of their own officers went abroad to study in European military schools. The military gained more respect. It served as one of the few institutions in Guatemala to provide social mobility. Few men from the lower classes actually rose into the middle and upper strata of society, but for the emerging middle class the Army became an avenue to prestige and power. The military included more than just the Army, as a National Police force also took on professional status. And eventually various government ministries and agencies had their own special police. These forces became instruments of strong-armed control by Guatemala's dictators almost to the end of the twentieth century. They were available to put down political and social disorder as well as ordinary crime, making the state safe for the development the Liberals wanted. Compulsory military service also enabled the Army to become a means of providing some education to the masses, especially along lines that would promote support for the modernization policies and national *esprit* behind the government. Moreover, the military began to provide useful services. The Military Hospital, for example, offered the best medical care available in Guatemala. By 1900 the military had been made responsible for construction and maintenance of roads and bridges and was also active in educational and other public-service programs.

If the military became the principal defender of Liberal governments, at the same time it also became the arbiter and destroyer of such governments. The stability that was so much a part of the ideal of the positivists who justified dictatorship was less characteristic of Guatemala than it was of Porfirio Díaz's Mexico. There were periods when instability and civil disturbances characterized Guatemala's politics. Factionalism, political and personal, within the military became intense, and it resulted in continual intrigue. With no check on its power, the Army could remove governments at will. Military chieftains jockeyed for power and position as alliances among commanding officers shifted. These personal relationships, tied to economic and family interests outside the Army, often obscured the ideological differences of political parties. In any case, by 1900 the old Conservative Party was gone and politics had become factional struggles within the Liberal Party.

Following the death of Barrios, the cabinet named a prominent merchant and friend of the fallen caudillo, Alejandro M. Sinibaldi, as temporary chief of state. Sinibaldi had been a Mayor of Guatemala City and a deputy to the National Assembly. With the Army in retreat from El Salvador, there was fear of a Salvadoran invasion and that Conservatives might take advantage of the situation to seize power. Sinibaldi thus granted extraordinary powers to the Minister of War, Martín Barrundia, son of José Francisco. Unable to conclude a peace with El Salvador, Sinibaldi resigned after only four days in office and on 7 April 1885 the Assembly named as provisional president General Manuel Lisandro Barillas, another native of Los Altos and one of Barrios's principal commanders in the Revolution of 1871. He had been *Jefe Político* of Quetzaltenango throughout the Barrios administration. Barillas successfully thwarted an attempt by Barrundia to seize power. Then, in November 1885, the Assembly elected Barillas to a six-year term, 1886–1892. Barillas released many of the political prisoners Barrios had jailed, but he also greatly increased the size of the Army and promoted many officers to General rank. Widespread corruption and military repression in response to several uprisings and rural unrest marred his administration. Only the rapid expansion of the coffee economy helped to mitigate the political instability of this military dictatorship.

General José María Reina Barrios, a nephew of Justo Rufino Barrios, won the presidential election easily in 1892. A native of Los Altos, like his uncle, Reina Barrios won popularity as a Liberal caudillo. In 1896 he granted amnesty to all those who had been exiled, seeking to heal the wounds of Guatemala's bitter Liberal-Conservative rivalry. By 1897, however, a serious economic downturn was contributing to rising opposition from within the Liberal Party. He ruthlessly crushed another attempted secession of Los Altos in the fall of 1897, after which the Assembly extended his six-year constitutional term for four more years, in the sort of *continuismo* that was becoming common in Central America. In this case, however, an assassin gunned him down on 8 February 1898. Later the same day the cabinet met and acknowledged Vice President Manuel Estrada Cabrera as his successor. An election later in the year confirmed Estrada Cabrera as president, and he won reelection in 1904, 1910, and 1916.

Manuel Estrada Cabrera

Of illegitimate parentage, and for that reason sometimes referred to derisively by his maternal surname (Cabrera), Guatemala's new dictator had worked hard in his native Quetzaltenango to establish himself as a lawyer and government bureaucrat strongly loyal to Barrios and his Liberal successors. Under Reina Barrios he served as Interior Minister, responsible for the internal government of the country, and Vice President. Many believed, however, that Estrada Cabrera may have been responsible for Reina Barrios' assassination. Nine years later, in 1907, former President Barillas, in exile in Mexico but involved in a plot to overthrow Estrada Cabrera, was also cut down by an assassin. Again, suspicion for directing this act fell on the Guatemalan president. Estrada Cabrera was skillful and brutal in maintaining his power against repeated attempted coups and attempts on his own life. His violent regime of 22 years (1898–1920) was the longest uninterrupted presidency in Guatemalan history.

While the regime became infamous for its brutality and corruption, it also was closely allied to the rise of the United Fruit Company's banana empire, as well as with the coffee elite.

The earthquakes that devastated Guatemala City in 1917 and 1918 contributed to rising opposition to the dictator, who did little to alleviate the widespread suffering. Falling coffee prices added to the economic decline. As elsewhere in Latin America at this time, student protests became a new factor in national politics and helped to awaken other elements of the populace. By 1920 a new political party, committed to Central American reunion, had unified many students, clergy, organized labor, and elements of an emerging middle class, to demand change. By this time, Estrada Cabrera was physically and mentally deteriorating and did not resist when the National Assembly declared him incompetent in April 1920. The Unionist Party's tenure in Guatemala, however, was short-lived. The Army, concerned over "subversive influence," in December 1921 imposed another Liberal military officer, General José María Orellana. After Orellana fell to a heart attack in 1926 another Liberal, General Lázaro Chacón, ruled the country until 1930. Nevertheless, despite continuing military rule in the 1920s, there was some relaxation of the political repression characteristic of earlier Liberal rule.

Cultural changes accompanied the Liberal Reforma, in large part the result of the decline of Church authority and removal of education from its domain, as well as the increasing foreign influence in the country. Guatemala fell far short of the stated Liberal goal of mass public education, but there was a drive to establish more schools at least for the urban middle class. A National Library, museums, academies, professional schools, and new universities opened. They emphasized scientific and technical studies, and they gave less attention to, and even opposed, the more traditional humanities. Expenditures for public education totaled nearly as much as that spent on the military, only service on the public debt ranked ahead of these two items in the annual budgets. That the state of education remained lamentably poor cannot be denied, but in relative terms the period witnessed great progress. Newspapers, magazines, and bookshops became more common. By 1895 Guatemala had thirty-three newspapers, including five dailies in the capital. Freedom of the press, if it did not become an absolute reality, at least became a political slogan that discouraged censorship or suppression of anti-government publications.

The indigenous peasants gained little from the new Liberals, who rejected the paternalism of the Conservatives while using the impoverished masses as the manpower for the material advances of their regimes. Through forced labor, vagrancy laws, and legalized debt peonage the poor were put to work on the plantations and roads. A system called the *mandamiento* virtually restored the colonial *repartimiento*, as indigenous villages supplied labor for both private and public works. The government seized much indigenous land when residents could not produce legal titles. Such land became available at low cost to planters, while the state forced inhabitants to seek wage employment on the land. The *mandamiento* formally ended with the Labor Code of 1894, but that law, far from protecting labor, was designed to "stimulate work" and "discourage vagrancy." It gave planters, under a contract system, extensive authority over workers and tacitly endorsed debt peonage. Laws that in theory emphasized the equality of all men actually went much further in protecting the employer than the employee. Most Guatemalans were virtual slaves to a system that worshiped material progress for a select few. Both on the farms and in urban establishments, six-day workweeks and 10- and 12-hour workdays were the norm. That such labor conditions were inefficient and characterized by low productivity and absenteeism sustained the notion that the Indians were lazy and shiftless. Landholders and bureaucrats who relentlessly exploited the helpless peasants had little comprehension of the necessity to provide adequate incentives and rewards or to provide channels by which the workers might improve their status through hard work.

Currency inflation further deteriorated standards of living during the period. Alcoholism became a major problem among the poor, if employer and government reports may be believed. Forced to provide for an expanding economy that provided economic and social benefits for only the middle and upper classes, cheap alcohol undoubtedly offered working-class people one of the few pleasures they could afford.

Armed troops ruthlessly suppressed efforts by Indians or workers to organize or strike. Local planters and employers, as well as local officials, had substantial police authority, and they imprisoned and punished workers who got out of line. Meanwhile, the government continued to grant land to planters so they could enlarge and develop coffee fincas and other plantations. Guatemala had considerable public land for such development, but in addition to this land there was the communal land of the Indians, upon which they steadily encroached. The government provided surveying either free or at a very low cost and protected privately-held titles at the expense of communally held lands.

The Liberals sought rapid material progress and, in large measure, they achieved that limited goal. They built roads, bridges, and ports, and they expanded agricultural production and exports. Yet they failed to achieve general prosperity. One landed oligarchy dedicated to traditional values simply gave way to another which, in league with foreign investors, reserved the advantages of modern civilization to itself. The social costs were very high. By the early twentieth century it was evident that the oligarchy shared control of the country with foreign planters, merchants, financiers, and diplomats. In order to attract investment and development to an area that had yet to prove its worth, the Liberals made exceedingly generous concessions. Foreign consuls encouraged and helped work out the details of such arrangements. Ever since the adoption of limited liability laws in the mid-nineteenth century, it had been possible for small companies to amass greater amounts of capital and look abroad for lucrative possibilities. Guatemala received such investments, but all too often the capitalization was insufficient to overcome the enormous obstacles to development in the region, and failure resulted. The instability of the government was one of the greatest obstacles, but natural obstacles were also important. A new oligarchy, based principally on producing and selling coffee to the wealthy nations, had political control, but it was a control that depended upon and had to be shared with foreign interests, increasingly typified by the great banana company.

The rise of bananas as a major export was closely related to the construction of railroads. While Guatemala had a railroad to the Pacific by 1880, the Caribbean watershed had proved more formidable. Construction there demanded either more capital or more cargo to make the railway return profits quickly, even before it was completed. The availability of rapid ocean steam navigation made possible the marketing of perishable bananas and other fruits in the United States and beyond. Banana companies gained concessions from Central American governments to build railroads that would carry their bananas to port quickly. Formation of the United Fruit Company (UFCO) in 1899 created a large corporate presence in Central America that established the International Railways of Central America (IRCA) as a subsidiary and in Guatemala completed the railroad from the Caribbean in 1908. In addition to the railroads, the UFCO had steamships. The "Great White Fleet" dominated service between Guatemala and the United States, an important part of the process by which U.S. economic interests replaced the British in the region. UFCO steamers became just about the only vessels serving Guatemala's north coast, and the company developed Puerto Barrios as Guatemala's principal port in the first half of the twentieth century.

UFCO extended its activities to make its primary operations more efficient. It pioneered radio communications between Central America and the United States, which led to the formation of another subsidiary, Tropical Radio & Telegraph Company, in 1913. It also controlled and enlarged the distribution process in the United States, which by 1950 consumed approximately 50 percent of the world's export of bananas. Later, UFCO expanded into food processing in Guatemala.

Unlike coffee, which was developed mostly by individual producers on small fincas, bananas became a giant foreign-controlled plantation crop. Profitable banana production needed large acreages, which it usually received by government grants. Eager for economic growth, the government of Estrada Cabrera conceded huge tracts of land to stimulate production, railroads, shipping, and port facilities. United Fruit not only marketed the produce of its own plantations; it also purchased bananas from smaller, independent producers. Since it controlled the market and transport, producers had little choice but to sell to the company at its price. This amounted to a virtual monopoly over production.

UFCO fulfilled the Guatemalan Liberal desire to develop the lowlands and to develop easier communication and transportation with the Caribbean and beyond. The government supplied the land, but in the sparsely-populated lowlands few workers from the highlands could be enticed to the hot, disease-ridden coastal plains. Thus, UFCO imported Jamaican and other West Indian blacks to provide a workforce for the plantations, railroad construction, docks, and other port facilities. This gave the north coast a substantially different ethnic composition from the highlands and this produced serious social tensions later. UFCO took the lead in eradicating yellow fever, malaria, and other tropical diseases, as well as taking measures against hookworm and other debilitating parasites. It set up clinics, inaugurated vaccination programs, and cooperated with international agencies and foundations in these efforts. Solution of these health problems was essential to the growth of the coastal region. Plant diseases and fungi were a further obstacle to development. Panama disease hit the banana plantations early in the century, and, beginning in 1935 a leaf spot disease called Sigatoka plagued the banana lands. Diseases and insects required a heavy investment in spraying, plant culture, and research. Moreover, hurricanes could devastate banana plantations. Such natural catastrophes underscored the reality that successful exploitation of tropical fruits required the ability to absorb heavy losses from time to time and thus the need for large land reserves.

UFCO's near monopoly on transportation led to resentment. Railroad rates were high and service poor. Steamship rates were the same, with lower rates from the United States to Guatemala than from Guatemala to the United States. Moreover, the improvement in international transportation failed to stimulate the hoped-for internal growth. Steamships, for example, connected Guatemala with the United States and Europe, but did not provide much service to other Central American ports. Before World War I German, Dutch, English, and Italian freighters shared the trade with the United States, but after 1914 North American shipping dominated the sea-lanes of Central America, particularly along the Caribbean shores, which had languished since the completion of the Panama Railway. UFCO favored its shipping line in a variety of ways. For example, its railway rates for hauling coffee were proportionately higher to the Pacific port of San José than to Puerto Barrios on the Caribbean, where UFCO ships could carry the cargo. Eventually, after World War II, UFCO made a concerted effort to improve its image in Guatemala and contributed generously to the educational, social, and cultural progress of the country.

German as well as U.S. economic interests replaced British domination in Guatemala. Although the North Americans had obvious geographical advantages, German initiative in the coffee industry, the growth of German shipping and manufacturing, and aggressive diplomacy made the Europeans formidable competitors. Yet despite the importance of Germans in coffee and North Americans in bananas, native Guatemalans retained control of much of the agriculture, and the new class of landlords that arose in collaboration with the Liberal governments and foreign investors lived comfortably. They depended, of course, on foreign markets, merchants, agents, and bankers. Moreover, foreigners took the lead in scientific farming, and the foreign-owned plantations generally produced higher yields than did native-owned plantations. Foreigners were highly important in financing native production. Foreign resident merchants and agents managed most of the international trade and even large-scale internal trade. By the twentieth century there were British, German, Dutch, U.S., French, and Middle Eastern merchants operating in Guatemala in significant numbers. After 1960 the Japanese also became influential. Before World War I the United States took the lead in this trade, while Great Britain fell behind Germany. The war temporarily displaced the Germans, but they recovered during the 1920s. The most consistent trend in the decades between the world wars, however, was the increasing share of the trade enjoyed by the United States. Even British Honduras came to be tied more closely to New Orleans than to Jamaica or Britain. Belize's location on the Central America-New Orleans banana route stimulated new investment in that tiny colony and resulted in new economic activity, although in general Belize remained depressingly poor.

Efforts to oust Estrada Cabrera, generally friendly to U.S. business interests, led to a joint U.S.-Mexican diplomatic venture in 1906. When El Salvador supported the Guatemalan revolutionaries, war resulted between the two countries. After Honduras joined El Salvador in the conflict, U.S. President Teddy Roosevelt tried unsuccessfully to end it through diplomacy. He then invited Mexican President Porfirio Díaz into a joint peacekeeping effort. Costa Rica joined Mexico and the U.S. in hosting a conference aboard the U.S.S. *Marblehead* at which all of the Central American states agreed to end hostilities, to stop abusing asylum, and to meet later in Costa Rica to work out a plan under which they would submit further disputes to the joint arbitration of the Mexican and U.S. presidents. Although Nicaragua refused to recognize the right of the United States to interfere in Central American affairs, the other four states reached accords that formed a basis for closer Central American cooperation, even if they did not succeed in completely ending the turmoil among the isthmian states. Mexican participation in this effort ended with the overthrow of Díaz in 1910 and U.S. prestige in the region diminished after its intervention in Nicaragua in 1912 and its continued military presence there into the 1930s. Although the U.S. did not intervene militarily in Guatemala, it made its influence felt. Under Woodrow Wilson especially, U.S. relations with Guatemala became more troubled. The U.S. State Department's intimation that it would not oppose Estrada Cabrera's overthrow was a factor in his ouster in 1920.

The Liberals who dominated the late nineteenth and early twentieth centuries had sacrificed political freedom to achieve material progress. The order which the positivists claimed should accompany the progress was noticeably missing in Guatemala. The military dictatorships, in collaboration with the coffee elite and foreign interests, made social change difficult, if not impossible. The Liberals had taken Guatemala out of its economic isolation and placed it unequivocally in the mainstream of neo-colonialism. The accompanying economic growth and modernization of Guatemala City and Quetzaltenango achieved some of the Liberal goals, but also hastened the growth of larger middle sectors who would not forever accept exclusion from the political process. Inevitably, as these sectors began to share the problems of economic growth, they demanded greater political and social privileges.

The gap between city and country widened as the capital lured those seeking employment and economic advance. Yet along with modern buildings, wide boulevards, monuments and parks, factories and airports, there arose huge slums around the outskirts and even within old sections of the capital. Control of epidemic diseases, improved medical care, and a corresponding drop in infant mortality led to rapid population growth. Caught in the revolution of rising expectations, these new city dwellers joined political and social movements. Denied adequate opportunities to achieve their expectations, they were open to persuasion by political demagogues. They were omnipresent reminders of the failure of the positivist development model to provide a general base of prosperity and progress.

New and rapid modes of public transportation—streetcars, later replaced by buses and mini-buses—supplemented by private motorcycles and automobiles, gave middle-class workers and professionals new mobility and freedom. Living patterns changed. The indoor bathroom became one of the major differences between rural and city living, between the middle and lower classes. The upper classes provided a thin veneer of culture and refinement in more traditional European terms. The emerging middle class worshiped the material culture that so characterized the positivist dream, often in imitation of the more garish aspects of U.S. life. Through expanding educational systems and communications, the children of peasants who had never been beyond the horizons of Sacatepéquez or Jutiapa now became aware of a larger world, of events in Europe and North America, of a glossy paradise to the north—at least as it was presented by Hollywood film-makers. Daily newspapers sprang up in profusion from the 1890s forward, many lasting only a short time, but others achieving popularity and respectability. Their circulations were small, but they had a major impact on Guatemalan thought. By the mid-1920s the leader was *Nuestro Diario*, with a circulation of about 4,000 daily, although the newly-formed *El Imparcial* would soon overtake it, and there were several other dailies.

The growth of leisure time activities among blue-collar and white-collar workers reflected the improved economic conditions. Bicycling, already important as a means of transportation, became a popular sport. Cyclists raced both in enclosed parks and cross-country over Guatemala's spectacular topography. European and North American cultural influence was evident here, too. Tennis and polo developed some popularity among the upper stratas as did golf, eventually, although soccer was much more popular among middle groups, both as a spectator and participants sport. Interest in bullfighting diminished in popularity and the Plaza de Toros in Guatemala, destroyed by the great earthquakes of 1917–1918, has never been rebuilt. There were occasional bullfights at major fairs or celebrations, but the activity lost the popularity it held in Spain, Colombia, or Mexico. Baseball, introduced as early as 1880, grew rapidly after 1900. Actively promoted by recreational programs of the United Fruit Company and by individuals of the U.S. business and diplomatic communities, it was taken up by amateurs. Eventually, professional baseball leagues appeared. Basketball and boxing also gained adherence, although the Guatemalans, most of whom are small in stature, did not achieve much notice in international competition. More recently, automobile racing has become popular. On the other hand, cockfighting diminished, although the gambling on which it had thrived continued as an important pastime for many.

Newspapers and magazines, later the radio, and still later television, contributed to a revolution in marketing and consumption. Advertising, as well as news and sports features, created appetites for a wider range of products. Most were imports from the United States or Europe, but the growing market created opportunities for a range of local manufactures. The expansion of cigarette smoking is an obvious example. Guatemalan men and even some women had long smoked cigars. In the early twentieth century, however, there was a massive increase in cigarette consumption, particularly among women. Advertising and U.S. cultural influence gradually broke down more traditional Hispanic and indigenous taboos regarding freedom of movement, sex, and morals. More employment opportunities became available to Guatemala's daughters, especially in government and business offices. Notwithstanding these changes, the women of Guatemala failed to achieve the rights and privileges that women in more developed nations gained before the mid-twentieth century.

Wider extension of credit was another aspect of the change taking place. Although Guatemala lagged far behind the United States in adopting wide-open credit plans, there was growing acceptance of installment buying, with both merchant and bank credit permitting greater consumption, particularly of larger appliances and housing. This in turn stimulated the construction industries, which helped to address the problem of the burgeoning urban populations. Suburban housing at a wide range of prices developed around the capital. Automobiles and traffic jams accompanied this centrifugal imitation of U.S. cities, particularly after World War II. Eventually Guatemala came to have a serious air pollution problem.

But not all Guatemalans enjoyed the new affluence accompanying the emergence of larger middle sectors. Not only did severe economic and social ills persist, they increased. In the urban slums, lacking the moral restraints of the rural communities, crime, illegitimacy, venereal diseases, and depressing poverty became serious problems. Health services failed to meet either the physiological or psychological needs of this population.

The small upper-class, spending considerable time abroad, did not patronize a tradition of artistic or cultural development comparable to that of the larger capitals of Latin America. Nevertheless, Guatemala's unique social and cultural ambience was fertile soil for some powerful literature and art. Especially representative of the period was the prolific Enrique Gómez Carrillo, although he was eventually eclipsed in importance by Miguel Ángel Asturias, who reflected Guatemalan themes especially well. Asturias became most well known for his *El Señor Presidente* (1946), the most famous of all Latin American "dictator novels." His other notable novels included *Leyendas de Guatemala* (1930), *Hombres de maíz* (1949), *Viento fuerte* (1950), *El Papa verde* (1954), and *Los ojos de los enterrados* (1960), but he also wrote poetry, plays, and journalistic articles. He received the Nobel Prize in 1967 "for his vivid literary achievement, deeply-rooted in national traits and traditions of Indian peoples."

Institutions of government served the interests of those who controlled the economy, often through harsh dictatorship, but always through a system that contradicted the constitutional phrases and campaign rhetoric about democracy and liberty. Political bosses held the keys to the system, and the principal political bosses were the chiefs of state. Those who wished to get ahead learned to play the game of bribery, influence, and family contacts. The excess of lawyers and law students reflected the willingness of the middle sectors to prepare themselves to play that game. Rigged elections or intimidation of the opposition secured the positions of the bosses. The Army was the arbiter, for it alone had the power to change the bosses. The positivistic professionalism in the military did not extend to non-interference in government. In fact, the military was one of the principal avenues for middle-class—and, occasionally, lower-class—elements to rise to higher positions in the country.

Two new groups, products of the Liberal reforms, began to appear in the early twentieth century and would make the political picture more complex: organized urban labor and university students and faculty. Estrada Cabrera viewed labor organization as subversive to the interests of capital growth and to peace and order. He suppressed strikes and labor demonstrations with armed force, while legislation that was progressive in the eyes of merchants, manufacturers, and foreign investors overlooked or actually repressed the rights of labor. But although the urban working class represented only a small percentage of Guatemala's total work force, its concentration in the capital made it more important politically than the scattered peasants of rural areas. Prior to 1920 the feeble labor organizations exercised slight influence, but after Estrada's overthrow a freer political atmosphere at least temporarily allowed labor to become more effective. Labor organization became identified with Marxism early and Central America's first Communist Party had appeared in Guatemala by 1924, demanding better labor legislation. The example of the Mexican Revolution was a powerful model for Guatemalan labor leaders as they sought both to improve working conditions and to influence the politics of the period. By the time of the Great Depression, urban labor constituted an incipient institutional force, rather closely identified with international Marxism.

University students also became a force in the 1920s as the natural result of the emphasis that the Liberals had put on education. The reorganized University of San Carlos became an essentially middle-class institution in the twentieth century. A few of the students were sons of urban working class, but most came from professional and propertied families. The wealthier members of society usually sent their children abroad for higher education. University education vastly accelerated middle class expectations, and it also brought home to them the glaring deficiencies, inequities, and injustices of Guatemalan society. Moreover, the Mexican and Russian Revolutions presented ideological alternatives to students who were searching for answers to Guatemala's problems. The university reforms begun in Córdoba, Argentina, in 1917 impacted the University of San Carlos. These reforms brought students closer to university administration, and they soon demanded recognition of university autonomy. The result was that the university became highly politicized. It was not only a forum for national politics, but—literally—a battleground at times. From the ranks of these students and intellectuals would come new political and labor leaders, influential journalists, and diplomats to champion social revolution. Not all were leftists, however, for fascism appealed to some. But they tended to agree that Guatemala needed government planning and direction of the economy, whether under a socialist system or one of managed capitalism. Intent on identifying their own cultural and political heritage, they assumed hostile attitudes toward the foreigners who dominated Guatemala. Their nationalism, often rooted in resentment, fear, frustration, and a sense of inferiority, was sometimes violent. Its effect on other elements of the populace was contagious.

Notwithstanding the increased emphasis on education, Guatemala remained one of the least literate countries in the Americas. Public education was especially weak, with shortages of books and teachers, and plagued by unimaginative teacher training and little contact with international pedagogical trends. Schools run by the foreign diplomatic and business communities—U.S., German, French, Italian, etc.—offered the best education, and children whose parents could afford them went to those schools. The Church, once so important in education, had a greatly diminished role, but one that did not disappear altogether. It continued to be an important moral force in some rural communities and among the wealthier classes in the cities. Indigenous *cofradías* (lay fraternities) continued to be important locally, but their ties to the Church grew tenuous as priests became scarce. To some degree, returning to the Church became a status symbol among the rising middle class. Increasingly numerous Protestant missions provided educational and health benefits in some areas, but their influence was local and did not bring general change.

While change in the capital was obvious, rural life in early twentieth-century Guatemala remained much as it had been a century earlier. Methods of cultivation changed little except for the export commodities, where coffee or bananas received scientific attention. The government cooperated with the landlords to maintain an inexpensive and docile labor force. Agricultural workers were severely exploited. Whereas a middle class was becoming apparent in the city, no such phenomenon occurred in rural areas.

The collapse of the western capitalist economies in 1929 had swift repercussions in Guatemala. Violence accompanied worker demonstrations and strikes. The barely discernible tendency trend toward democratic processes during the 1920s met a sharp reaction as a result of the hardship accompanying the Great Depression. General Jorge Ubico Castañeda became the military dictator in 1931 and branded all attempts toward social reform as "communist." He dealt brutally with anyone who challenged his rule, but the utter inability of the government to cope with the economic problems led to greater faith among elites in authoritarian rule. Many felt the lure of the fascist examples of Spain and Italy. Fear of Communist agitation caused the elite to question democratic liberalism, enabling Ubico to build his dictatorship quickly. Elected freely in 1931, he moved swiftly to restore peace and order, absorbing most of the authority of the government into the executive branch. In 1932 he launched a vicious war on the Communists. He ordered ten of them executed, including Juan Pablo Wainwright, a Honduran Communist organizer who had led a strike of UFCO banana workers. Refugees from the unsuccessful leftist revolt in El Salvador of the same year suffered imprisonment. The purge peaked in 1934 when Ubico uncovered and crushed unmercifully a plot against himself. A wave of assassinations, executions, long prison terms, and exiles removed all opposition. *Time Magazine* quoted Ubico as saying, "I have no friends, only domesticated enemies." The campaign destroyed the Communist Party of Guatemala. Those leaders who were not killed, fled the country or stayed out of sight. Other opposition parties were neutralized as effectively. Labor organizations suffered a similar fate. The government disbanded trade unions and executed or exiled their leaders. A leftist labor organization continued to operate underground, but by 1940 it was no more than a skeleton organization, with most of its leaders in Mexico or El Salvador. Reelected periodically in controlled elections, Ubico became one of Central America's classic right-wing dictators of the 1930s. Officially "Liberal," it more closely resembled the fascism of Spain, Italy, and other Latin American dictatorships of the era.

With the opposition silenced, Ubico stabilized the Guatemalan economy. His government was efficient, and it greatly improved Guatemala's credit, chiefly by granting favorable concessions to foreign, particularly U.S. and German, enterprises. Although Ubico's policies built up the national treasury and credit abroad, they did little for the average worker. Extensive public works projects employed forced labor, while foreigners enjoyed privileges unknown to most Guatemalans. Symbolic of his government's focus, in 1934 Ubico transferred the Department of Labor from the Development Ministry to the supervision of the National Police. Working conditions deteriorated and real wages declined.

Through demagoguery and patronage, Ubico cultivated support among the agrarian working class. His political machine relied on occasional popular support among Guatemala's indigenous peoples. He reduced the power of the landlords over the peasants by abolishing debt slavery, while at the same time he increased government control over labor. A vagrancy law assured a supply of labor to the coffee planters, but Ubico's political bosses were able to control that labor force so that it might be used for government projects, or, more to the point, as a means of intimidating landowners. Growing pressure from international organizations finally prompted a minimum wage law in July 1943, but it is doubtful that it made much difference. The real standard of living for rural Guatemalans remained deplorably low.

Ubico, a few Guatemalans, and the foreigners profited handsomely, and they banked their money in the United States or Europe. A garrison of ragged National Police kept order in each village under the orders of a local superintendent or departmental governor. Crimes against foreigners earned swift and harsh punishment. An efficient secret service under the direction of General Roderico Anzueto kept the dictator informed of nascent plots or organized resistance. Anti-intellectual and fearful of innovation, Ubico prohibited discussion of Guatemala's problems or social structure. The material improvements, the hundreds of miles of new roads, and the diplomatic victories in disputes over sparsely populated border areas were relatively minor gains when so few enjoyed their advantages.

Liberal development of Guatemala had continued almost unabated since 1871, but it was soon to end. The Liberals had achieved considerable modernization, although Guatemala still lagged behind much of the rest of Latin America in social and economic development. Yet the middle and working classes had been awakened and were beginning to challenge the exclusive domination of politics by the oligarchy. The oligarchy had thus turned more and more to the military to protect their privileged status. This allowed the military to become a powerful institutional power in its own right.

7

The Ten Years of Spring

Juan José Arévalo

Significant changes had begun to occur in Guatemala before the end of World War II. The middle and working classes had begun to participate in the society, effecting permanent alterations in ruling patterns. Maintaining the Ubico dictatorship required increased repression amid growing signs of unrest. Active opposition surfaced in 1941, when university students cheered the lone member of the National Assembly who dared to vote against extending Ubico's tenure in office to 1949. Later, the students became bolder and began to demonstrate in support of demands for changing university administration. A group composed primarily of law students calling themselves the *Esquilaches* (apparently in reference to the 1766 Madrid revolt) met secretly to plot against the regime. Led by Mario Méndez Montenegro, the Esquilaches included several men who would later play major leadership roles: José Manuel Fortuny, Jorge Luis Arriola, Manuel Galich, Julio César Méndez Montenegro, and Mario Efraín Nájera Farfán.

Ubico, despite his openly pro-German sentiments, had opportunistically joined Guatemala's neighbors in declaring war against the Axis powers. He cooperated with U.S. agents in reducing German influence and economic power to the extent of confiscating German property and removing suspected Nazi-sympathizers to detention camps in Texas. The anti-fascist propaganda—including the Atlantic Charter and the wartime alliance with the Soviet Union—that entered the country undermined Ubico's hold, especially in the capital. In 1942 Guatemalan workers and university students demonstrated in sympathy with a Salvadoran revolt against the Liberal dictator Maximiliano Hernández-Martínez. When, two years later, Hernández fled El Salvador and sought exile in Guatemala, there were even larger manifestations of protest. Here was the beginning of the alliance among students, military officers, and workers that finally ousted Ubico. Spontaneous acceptance of student leadership characterized urban labor's opposition to the dictator. Ubico's recognition of the rising cost of living was inadequate. The 1943 minimum wage law was a mere gesture, and it fell far short of winning support from the urban workers. They continued to demonstrate.

Ubico responded by giving a salary increase of 15 percent to all government employees earning $150 or less monthly. This measure may have won the loyalty of government workers, but it alienated others, who received no corresponding raise. On 22 June 1944 he accused students of promoting Nazi-fascist ideas, withdrew constitutional guarantees, and tightened the military rule over the country. This action led immediately to the series of strikes that brought about Ubico's resignation.

While workers and students battled police in the streets, Mario Nájera Farfán led a few professional men in the secret formation of the National Renovation Party (PRN). They agreed to support exiled university professor Juan José Arévalo Bermejo for president. At about the same time a group of university students founded the Popular Liberation Front (FPL) and joined the crusade against Ubico, claiming adherence of 85 percent of the registered students. A third party, the Social Democrats (PSD), later resulted from a factional split within the FPL. These political factions had in common their desire to end the dictatorship and to replace it with a more egalitarian government, one which would modernize the country's institutions, integrate the indigenous peoples, encourage the growth of labor and peasant movements, and promote advanced social legislation and economic growth.

Railroad workers halted the country's transportation on 26 June. More workers joined in what became a general strike. Ubico capitulated on 1 July, turning over power to a triumvirate of officers headed by Federico Ponce Vaides. Ubico's failing health undoubtedly contributed to his decision to step down. Seeking modern medical care, he went into exile in New Orleans, where he died two years later.

General Ponce, who had a reputation for cruelty, was potentially as dictatorial as Ubico, but the force of public opinion compelled him to restore constitutional guarantees, promise a national election in November, and permit the existence of political parties and labor unions as a condition to restarting the economy. Ponce did not yield easily to further demands. He quartered a detachment of mounted, machete-brandishing Indians at the outskirts of the capital as "proof" that he had indigenous support for his government. These troops effectively broke up mass demonstrations. The press had become bolder in its criticism of the government once Ubico was gone, but on 1 October police agents, reportedly on Ponce's orders, assassinated Alejandro Córdova, the respected founder and director of Guatemala's leading daily, *El Imparcial*. Violence followed. Then, before dawn on 20 October, 70 students and workers under the command of Major Francisco J. Arana took the fortress of the Guardia de Honor and from there distributed arms to other students and workers. By sunrise revolutionaries were in command of the city except for the recently constructed (1942) and heavily defended National Palace, which they threatened to bombard with artillery. The foreign diplomatic corps helped organize a new government, which was installed by five o'clock the same afternoon.

The revolutionary junta, consisting of Arana, Captain Jacobo Arbenz Guzmán, and Jorge Toriello Garrido (a prominent merchant), governed until 15 March 1945, when Dr. Arévalo, elected in a landslide in December 1944, took office.

Arévalo, who had been teaching philosophy in Argentina, projected a political ideology he called "spiritual socialism." He did not ignore material matters, but stressed the dignity of man, national independence, and freedom of spirit. "Our socialism does not aim at ingenious distribution of material goods," he declared soon after his return to Guatemala. "Our socialism aims to liberate men psychologically, to return it to all the psychological and spiritual integrity that has been denied them by conservatism and liberalism." This doctrine of psychological and moral liberation meant for Guatemala a reform program that would challenge the oligarchy and the foreign domination of the country. In his inaugural address Arévalo announced a policy of sympathy for the worker and the peasant. "We shall give civic and legal value to all people who live in this Republic," he declared. Moreover, schools would henceforth "carry not only hygiene and literacy," but also "the doctrine of revolution."

Ubico's fall opened the way for the return of exiles and foreigners who were influential in organizing labor unions and political factions. They infused a leftist tone to the labor movement. Under the leadership of the young and dynamic Víctor Manuel Gutiérrez, the teachers' union became the key to Communist control of urban labor and to formation of a Central Labor Federation (CTG) in 1944. The CTG affiliated with the pro-Communist Confederation of Latin American Workers (CTAL) and by 1950 Communist leaders were well established in Guatemalan trade unions. The CTG headquarters became a center for returning exiles and foreign labor organizers, who helped train and organize Guatemalan labor leaders. By August 1944 the Communists had already formed the National Vanguard Party, which met secretly until 1949 when it publicly became the Communist Party of Guatemala (PCG).

Labor's new status found expression in the Constitution of 1945, a modern document patterned closely after the Mexican Constitution of 1917. A new Labor Code guaranteed workers the right to organize and strike and provided for collective bargaining, minimum wages, and a long list of other tangible benefits. It required employers to provide proper housing, schooling, and medical care for workers, and to pay indemnities of a month's salary for each year's employment to any worker discharged without just cause. The code also defined responsibility for regulation of labor unions, development of cooperatives and inexpensive housing, and arbitration of labor disputes, including the establishment of special Labor Tribunals. A political action group (CNUS) within the CTG succeeded in accelerating the rate of social reform by committing the government to the objectives of organized labor, rural as well as urban. The Labor Tribunals almost always decided cases in favor of labor on the basis of the clause of the Labor Code stating that "private interests must yield to the social or collective interests."

The overthrow of the Liberal dictatorship also represented a generational change. The revolutionaries—students, professionals, labor leaders, and military officers—were mostly younger people resentful toward the aging army officers and Liberal politicians who had surrounded Ubico. Arévalo and the new national congress reflected the victory of youth in the Revolution and would quickly advance revolutionary legislation uninhibited by the constraints of tradition or vested interest.

Backed by substantial portions of the urban middle and lower classes, Arévalo pursued a program that promised structural change. The new Constitution empowered all males and literate females over the age of 18 to vote. It opened the way for much greater self-government at the local level, replacing the centralized control of the Liberal era. An expanded educational program attacked the country's staggering (75 percent) illiteracy, while the government, through improvements in health services and disease control, tried to cope with the immense physical problems. In October 1946 Arévalo's government established the Guatemalan Social Security Institute (IGSS) that provided workmen's compensation, and began a system of social security and health care. An Institute for the Development of Production (INFOP) worked to expand productivity, particularly in small manufacturing and processing industries, by supplying credit and technical assistance. Discussion of agrarian reform followed the urban reforms, but Arévalo's government did not move very far in that direction, cognizant of the power of the coffee and banana interests.

Arévalo's support of labor and peasant demands and his "softness" toward the Communists brought him, nevertheless, into direct conflict with the defenders of the old order—the planters and foreign investors who feared losing the advantages secured under Ubico. They believed that the welfare state, labor unions, higher wages, social insurance, and increased taxes would wreck the economy—and more precisely, their own interests.

The Roman Catholic Church also became a dedicated foe of the Guatemalan Revolution. With Church power apparently broken, Ubico had relaxed the anticlericalism of his Liberal predecessors and allowed the Church to recover some of it former strength, without formally reversing the restraints on clerical activity imposed by the Constitution of 1879. Catholic clerics hoped that Ubico's overthrow might offer an opportunity to restore the rights and privileges they had enjoyed before the Liberal Reforma, but leaders of the Revolution of 1944 quickly made it clear that they had no intention of reversing the Liberal anticlerical reforms. The arrival of many Spanish priests, fresh from the Spanish Civil War of the 1930s, reenforced the Conservative character of the Guatemalan clergy. By 1944 a quarter of the 273 parish priests in Guatemala were Spaniards. Ubico also allowed Maryknoll missionaries expelled from China to come into Guatemala in 1943, although he prohibited them from engaging in political activities. The Maryknollers, however, would later come to represent a more progressive element of Guatemalan Catholicism. Under Ubico, too, nuns and priests returned to teaching in private schools. Other clergy became involved in indigenous education and in hospitals. These actions, as well as permitting wearing of religious garb in public, clearly violated the Constitution of 1879. Ubico developed a cordial relationship with the staunchly conservative Archbishop Mariano Rossell y Arellano, in contrast to the expulsions of higher clergy that earlier Liberal presidents had ordered. Rossell himself had been exiled in 1922 with Archbishop Luis Javier Muñoz y Capurón for whom he had been secretary. In the 1930s, however, Ubico and Rossell shared a hatred for Communism as well as a respect for Spanish dictator General Francisco Franco. Ubico had benefitted from the fascist propaganda of the Spaniards in Guatemala, but after 1944 the Church would pay a price for its close association with the Spanish Falangists.

Following Arévalo's election, Catholic publications were quick to criticize the new president, especially after the new Constitution retained the anticlerical provisions of the 1879 Constitution. A new Catholic newspaper, *Acción Social Cristiana*, from 1 February 1945 forward carried on a hostile campaign toward the government and the Revolution, increasingly identifying the government with Communism. A Catholic radio station later supplemented this and other similar attacks from the Catholic press. Although Arévalo proclaimed freedom of speech in Guatemala, his government eventually shut down Catholic radio and print media, accusing them of promoting lies among the uneducated population. Archbishop Rosell Arellano led the attack and became symbolic of the Church's opposition to Arévalo and the Revolution, referring to the 1945 Constitution as "communistic." The declining number of priests in the country, however, reflected the weakness of the Church's position. Many of the Spaniards left Guatemala after 1945, so that by 1949 there were only 130 priests in the entire country.

Some Army officers believed that only a military administration could govern the country effectively. Many younger officers had supported the Revolution, but others were still closely tied to the coffee elite. Moreover, Arévalo's efforts to scale back the military, including abolishing any future promotions to the rank of general, had rankled senior officers. Arévalo weathered at least twenty-two military revolts during his five years in office. The loyalty of his Chief of the Armed Forces, Colonel Francisco Arana, had been vital to the survival of Arévalo's government, but by 1948 Arana was increasingly identified with right-wing politicians. In November of that year the Congress formally censured him for conspiring to interfere with congressional elections. Arana denied that charge, but by mid-1949 Arévalo suspected Arana of plotting against him. Arana was the principal rival to Defense Minister Jacobo Arbenz for the presidency in the upcoming 1950 election. The Constitution prohibited re-

Jacobo Arbenz campaigning for the presidency in 1950

Courtesy of Oscar Peláez Almengor
and the Universidad de San Carlos de Guatemala

election. After consultation with Arbenz, Arévalo conspired to arrest Arana. It may never be known for certain whether, on 18 July near Amatitlán, Arévalo's police were merely attempting to arrest Arana and shot him when he attempted to escape, as they claimed, or whether it was a deliberate assassination. In either case, the apparent conspiracy between Arévalo and Arbenz in eliminating the more conservative Arana left the way open for Arbenz's election the following year.

A new military revolt followed Arana's death. The government issued arms to some workers, and they aided significantly in the suppression of this revolt, but the Army remained the principal threat to government.

At the other extreme, a small but militant group of students, editors, and other intellectuals wanted a more thoroughgoing social revolution. The Communists feared that Arévalo's program, although it coincided with their own in some respects, could not be made to conform to their Marxist conceptual approach and that it might pose a threat to their own party's establishment as sole leader of the proletariat. As the election of 1950 approached, the Communists campaign more openly. Led by José Fortuny, seventeen Communists withdrew from Arévalo's Revolutionary Action Party (PAR) and began to publish a procommunist weekly, *Octubre*. Arévalo, anxious not to lose his moderate support, responded with a tougher line toward the Communists, but the presence of Communists in key government information organs gave them a big advantage. Several worked in the government news bureau. Another had been manager of the Board of Directors of the government's radio station since 1946. The official government daily, *Diario de Centroamérica*, reflected a leftist bias, and in 1949 Alfredo Guerra Borges, one of the country's leading journalists and a member of the Communist Party's Executive Committee, became its editor. The semi-official *Nuestro Diario* also came under Communist management about 1948.

Arbenz was a member of the National Renovation Party—which joined with the PAR (Arévalo), the FPL, the Revolutionary Party of National Union (PRUN), and the Communists—in presenting a united coalition (Unidad Nacional) of moderate and leftist parties. The principal opposition came from conservative parties, National Redemption and the Anti-Communist Union, supporting Ubico's former director of public works, General Miguel Ydígoras Fuentes, who also received the endorsement of Archbishop Rossell. The government hardly permitted free campaigning, even though Arbenz would likely have won a free election. A government arrest order forced Ydígoras into hiding. Arbenz won with an overwhelming majority.

Under Arbenz, Guatemala moved sharply toward the left and into a friendlier relationship with the Soviet Union. In an effort to widen their popular support and overcome differences between Stalinists and Guatemalan Nationalists, the Communists reorganized in 1952 as the Guatemalan Labor Party (PGT). This party promoted mass organizations that pressured the government on behalf of agrarian reform, collectivization, and a foreign policy that criticized the U.S. intervention in Korea and praised the U.S.S.R. Agrarian Reform became the centerpiece of Arbenz's administration beginning in 1952. Although the policy sought peasant support, the government actually concentrated on the vast foreign banana holdings of the lowlands rather than on the native-owned coffee fincas in the populous highlands. The whole concept of land redistribution, however, planted fear among Guatemalan landlords and brought them more actively to oppose the revolutionary reforms.

As opposition mounted toward Arbenz, urban labor was his primary source of strength. Labor unions and other mass organizations attacked the opposition, first with propaganda, later with more violent tactics. Those considered enemies of the government suffered arrest, imprisonment, torture, and assassination. There was a startling increase of attacks against centers of anti-

Communist activity by groups of masked hoodlums. This sort of paramilitary action in support of the government was not new in Guatemalan history, and it would not end with the Arbenz government, but it tended to discredit the democratic aims that the Revolution had proclaimed.

The Communists realized that the Army, mostly non-Communist and increasingly suspicious of Arbenz, was the principal obstacle to a more thoroughgoing Marxist revolution. Arévalo had armed some workers during the 1949 insurrection. In 1952, as tension surrounded passing of the Agrarian Reform Law, leftists favored formation of armed "defense brigades" within the labor movement. The government refused to do this, but as fear of foreign intervention rose in 1954, labor leaders repeated the idea. Ernesto ("Che") Guevara, a recent Argentine arrival employed in the Agrarian Reform Department, urged that the labor unions be armed at once, but Arbenz, himself a military officer, was reluctant. Yet the Army's fear of such action was a principal cause for its early repudiation of Arbenz during the subsequent invasion. Arbenz had reduced military spending to ten percent of the national budget. It had been seventeen percent under Ubico. The Communist-controlled labor unions also played a role beyond Guatemala's borders and the PGT was a center for propaganda and agitation in the neighboring states. *Octubre* reflected an identification of interests between Guatemalan and other Central America workers. Then, in 1954 Guatemalan workers joined Hondurans in a strike against the United Fruit Company on the north coast of Honduras. Guatemalan labor unions also aided Salvadoran workers in labor actions.

Yet Guatemala was not a Communist state in 1954. Arbenz himself did not openly profess communism, although his Salvadoran wife, María Cristina Villanova, was an active member of the PGT and Communists had easy access to the President. They held key positions in all three branches of the government, which had begun to expropriate large landholdings, particularly those of the United Fruit Company. Implementation of the Agrarian Reform Law had begun a restructuring of the Guatemalan economy, society, and political life, but it was far from completed. Guatemala had remained a fundamentally capitalist country. The reforms of the Guatemalan Revolution, far from aiming at establishment of a Communist regime, had sought to encourage a more modern capitalism that included social benefits and incentives for the entire population. The Revolution, however, was also nationalistic and it aroused the anti-foreign sentiments that had been suppressed during nearly a century of Liberal rule.

Speeches of the Guatemalan delegates to the United Nations as well as official statements of the Guatemalan government suggested that, insofar as foreign policy was concerned, Guatemala had become a virtual Soviet satellite by 1954. UFCO had been actively criticizing Guatemala's "red" government since the late 1940s, making it a Cold War issue in the United States. When Guatemalan exiles from Honduras, assisted by U.S. Marine Corps and CIA advisers, invaded the country, the Guatemalan army refused to defend the government, precipitating a crisis. Later, revolutionaries in Cuba and Nicaragua would learn from the Guatemalan experience the importance of eliminating the armed forces of the old order and restructuring the society as quickly as possible with a loyal revolutionary armed force. Despite mounting opposition, it is unlikely that the Arbenz government would have fallen if all or most of the military had not defected.

Guatemala demonstrated just how far a small Caribbean republic could go in challenging the hegemony of U.S. economic interests. Right wingers—including the U.S. Ambassador to Guatemala, Richard Patterson—had warned against the Marxist tendencies of the Arévalo government, but the Truman administration did no more than keep a half-open eye on Guatemala, although in February 1952 it authorized the CIA to plan covert operations there. Meanwhile, United States investments and profits in the republic rose rapidly after World War II. Despite the activities of Communists and other leftist, the actual practices of the Arévalo government had not seemed to threaten those interests seriously. Even during the first two years of the Arbenz regime there was little official United States concern expressed.

With the Eisenhower administration, however, and with John Foster Dulles as Secretary of State, Washington had suddenly became more keenly aware of a Soviet challenge in Guatemala. Dulles had close connections with the United Fruit Company. Arbenz's pro-labor policies also threatened other business interests, notably Pan American World Airways. After the Guatemalan government had in March 1950 expelled Ambassador Patterson for meddling in Guatemala's internal affairs, Truman had named Rudolph Schoenfield to represent the U.S. there. Schoenfield was also a harsh critic of Arbenz, but in 1953 the new U.S. President, Dwight Eisenhower, named John E. Peurifoy as Ambassador. Dulles believed Peurifoy, also outspoken in his criticism of the Guatemalan government, to be better trained to participate in the intervention that would oust Arbenz in 1954. The pro-Soviet stance of Guatemala in the United Nations was an embarrassment to the fanatically anti-Communist Republicans around Dulles, and he chose to end the "Good Neighbor" policy of non-intervention that Franklin Roosevelt had inaugurated twenty years earlier.

The pro-Soviet and anti-American declarations of the Guatemalans had by 1953 elicited strong reactions in the U.S. Extravagant eulogies from the Guatemalan press and Congress upon the death of Joseph Stalin, for example, prompted virulent verbal attacks in the United States on the Guatemalan government, with calls for intervention to suppress Communism there. The United States news media began to increase its coverage of the "red regime" in Guatemala. Dulles attempted to get strong inter-American backing for an intervention, but the watered-down resolutions against international communism at Caracas in March

1954 lacked the support of several major Latin American states. Those nations hardly sanctioned the sort of unilateral intervention that the United States sponsored in June. Meanwhile, the mounting internal opposition to Arbenz solidified when Archbishop Rossell y Arellano on 10 April called for Guatemalans to rise up and throw out the Communists.

Alarmed over the arrival in May of Czechoslovakian arms at Puerto Barrios aboard the Swedish ship *Alfhem*, the United States determined to act. The CIA directed the operation known as "El Diablo." The CIA had already been planning a covert operation under the code name Operation "PBSuccess," authorized by Eisenhower in August 1953, including developing a list of some 58 persons in Guatemala targeted for assassination. Two Guatemalan exiles, General Ydígoras and Colonel Carlos Castillo Armas had already organized a plan for invasion. The United States, under hastily signed military security treaties, airlifted arms into Honduras and Nicaragua. Then those governments cooperated in outfitting the invasion force. U.S. planes dropped anti-Arbenz leaflets over Guatemala City and clandestine radio broadcasts warned of a large invasion that would come soon, creating a climate of fear and apprehension in Guatemala.

The United States waited until its delegate, Henry Cabot Lodge, Jr., was President of the United Nations Security Council during the month of June. The invasion by the Guatemalan exile force began on 18 June. When Guatemala protested, Lodge put off calling a meeting until 25 June and then obstructed the placing of the Guatemalan case on the agenda, arguing that the Organization of American States (OAS) should take up the matter first. Meanwhile, in Guatemala, the Army refused to resist the invasion, and Castillo Armas soon controlled the country. Arbenz resigned on 27 June and quickly left for Mexico. Later he went to Cuba and Europe before returning to Mexico City, where he died mysteriously in 1971.

The delay of international organizations in responding to the intervention precluded effective action on their part. The Inter-American Peace Committee of the OAS did not even convene until two days after Arbenz's resignation, and it accomplished nothing. An interim government attempted to salvage the Revolution, but two days later turned over control to anti-Communist Colonel Elfego Monzón. Monzón met with Castillo in San Salvador on the following day (30 June), and on 8 July Castillo became head of the junta they had established.

Aside from the political changes that the Guatemalan Revolution had brought, it had achieved by 1954 significant economic and social modernization of the country. In part owing to the substantial improvements in sanitation and public health the population had grown from approximately 2.4 million in 1944 to 3.3 million by 1954. Although partly accounted for by the rapid inflation of the post-war years, Guatemala's Gross National Product (GNP) had soared from \$131.6 million in 1943 to \$558.3 million by 1953, an annual per capita jump from \$55.6 to \$180.5 for that period. The value of exports had risen from slightly more than \$20 million in 1943 to nearly \$108 million by 1953 and government revenues for the same period from \$14.7 million to \$65.3 million.[1] The Agrarian Reform Law had redistributed a relatively small amount of land, but had been at the center of a government commitment to improving the well being of the rural inhabitants and to restructuring Guatemala better to reflect middle and lower class interests. Guatemala was clearly becoming more prosperous and more socially equitable. The revolutionary goals of democracy, justice, and economic growth, if not totally fulfilled, were clearly making progress be-

[1] From *Memoria del Banco de Guatemala*, 1953, 1954, and *Estudio económico para América Latina*, 1953, as cited by Jim Handy, *Gift of the Devil: A History of Guatemala* (Boston: South End Press, 1984), p. 129.

fore the overthrow of Arbenz. Caught up in the Cold War, with which it had little to do initially, the Guatemalan Revolution had also alienated powerful segments of the country—the Army, the coffee oligarchy, the Church, and foreign enterprise—which would successfully conspire with the United States to end the ten years of Spring.

8

The Thirty Years War

Efraín Ríos Montt

Following a plebiscite in October 1954, Castillo Armas ruled Guatemala as President until his assassination in 1957. Castillo had already moved promptly to eliminate all Communist influence from Guatemala. A National Committee for Defense against Communism supervised a repressive purge. On 10 August 1954 he disbanded all political parties. A "Political Statute" decreed on the following day replaced the Constitution of 1945, authorized Castillo's military rule of the country, outlawed the Communist Party, and banned Communist books and propaganda. A wave of arrests, assassinations, and exiles followed. Although Arbenz and his top aides were able to flee the country, the new government rounded up and killed hundreds of people, a harbinger of the brutal policies of successive military governments for the next thirty years when, according to human rights organizations, more than 100,000 civilians died at the hands of government paramilitary squads. In an effort to recover funds that Arbenz and other government officials had taken from the treasury upon their departure, Castillo confiscated the property of some 80 former government officials.

Although reactionary in many respects, the Castillo government and those that succeeded it did not totally dismantle the Guatemalan Revolution. Many of the institutions that Arévalo had inaugurated remained, even though their impetus toward social restructuring ended. The government could not ignore entirely the popularity of leftist social and political reforms among workers, peasants, and intellectuals, so it attempted to maintain the appearance of reform and progressive legislation. Although it quickly repealed some acts of the Arévalo and Arbenz years, it then superseded or amended many more to prevent the intended restructuring.

Labor's influence in government ended. A "right to work" law checked organized labor further in 1956. A new Constitution in 1956 reflected the anti-Communism of the era when it forbade all "foreign intervention" in the labor movement. An Agrarian Reform Law, passed in 1956, provided for expropriation and redistribution of idle land, but the specific terms of the act left the landed class with little to fear. The Church also regained some of its lost privileges, the most important of which was the right to all property that it had lost following the Revolution of 1871.

In short, the old Liberal elites—the coffee planters and other landholders, as well as the foreign capitalists and their subsidiaries—returned to power, protected by the military regimes. In fact, the elite classes in Guatemala had become much larger as the economy had expanded. In addition to coffee and bananas, there had grown up a significant industrial elite, as well as other economic groups that had achieved varying degrees of success. Thus it was no longer accurate to refer to the dominant class as merely an oligarchy, for there were in fact several different elites in the country that now competed and collaborated for government favor. Yet for the next three decades, the most obvious elite that dominated the country's government was the military establishment. The officer corps thrived during these years and expanded both its political and economic positions. In economic policy the military governments of the next three decades returned Guatemala to the policies that had guided the Liberals from 1871 to 1944. These Neo-Liberals would increasingly be regarded as "conservative" in U.S. terminology. Whatever they were called, they were decidedly more favorable to the interests of the business and agroexport sectors than to those of the working poor.

Although voices of moderation occasionally prevailed, it was clear that interests antagonistic to the social revolution had recovered control. But they could not suppress all opposition. Student demonstrations were especially vocal after 1954. The government often used force to suppress them. The Army was the real master of the country, as it had been before 1944. Castillo Armas thoroughly reorganized the officer corps in 1956 and purged any officers still loyal to Arbenz. After Castillo's assassination by one of his palace guards in July 1957, Guatemala suffered a period of unstable governments, and widespread terrorism and intimidation of more progressive candidates accompanied elections. General Ydígoras had expected to succeed Castillo as a reward for his part in the Arbenz's overthrow. When he did not, the Army intervened, and in January 1958 it held elections that Ydígoras won.

Once in office, Ydígoras made an effort to unify the country and was conciliatory toward moderate leftist elements, but these efforts only got him into trouble with his conservative allies. Whenever free elections were held at local levels in the capital, the electorate expressed broad preference for leftists, such as Luis Fernando Galich López, who was elected Mayor in 1959 after various attempts to deny him that office failed. Fidel Castro's establishment of a leftist revolutionary regime in Cuba further polarized public opinion in Guatemala. Violence flared frequently in 1960, as Ydígoras, seeking to widen his popularity, was reluctant to resort to harsh measures against the opposition, while at the same time he supported maneuvers to deny his opponents access to power through democratic means. Ydígoras provided Cuban exiles with a base near Retalhuleu, where, under the supervision of U.S. military personnel, they trained for the ill-fated Bay of Pigs invasion of Cuba that would occur in April 1961. In November 1960, Ydígoras put down a serious revolt, led by Colonel Rafael Pereira, which broke out at the Matamoros Barracks in the capital. Other rebels invaded from Cuba, advancing inland as far as Zacapa before Ydígoras, personally leading his forces and supported by his air force's B-26 bombers, turned them back.

Although Pereira's threat failed, it was the beginning of a new phase of Guatemala's revolutionary history, as survivors of the rebellion, led by Lieutenant Marcos Aurelio Yon Sosa, formed the Thirteenth of November Revolutionary Movement (MR-13) and began a guerrilla war that continued for three decades. Another officer, Luis Turcios Lima, later formed a rival guerrilla group, the Rebel Armed Forces (FAR), that collaborated with the outlawed, underground PGT. These guerrillas kept Guatemala in a state of turmoil throughout the 1960s. Although they failed to control much territory, they created a sense of insecurity in the country and were aided by substantial support from middle-class youth in the university and even had some support from disgruntled younger officers within the Army. A right-wing terror organization, the White Hand (*Mano Blanca*), arose in response, and assassination and terrorism spread. Later, another organization, known as the Eye for an Eye (*Ojo por Ojo*), replaced the Mano Blanca when that group's close relationship to the government and police became embarrassing. After Turcios died in an automobile collision, César Montes emerged as a new and more dynamic leader of the FAR.

The return of leftist exiles, including Arévalo, Fortuny, and Gutiérrez, raised the political tension in Guatemala. Arévalo's announcement that he would be a candidate for the presidency incited a strong right-wing reaction. Ydígoras's failure to pursue a hard enough line against these "agitators" led senior military officers suddenly to remove him from office in March 1963.

Among Ydígoras' achievements was closer collaboration with the other Central American states on matters of defense, trade, and cultural development. Such efforts, which some hoped optimistically might lead to restoration of Central American political union, had begun during the Arévalo and Arbenz years. Guatemala had joined with the other Central American nations to form the Organization of Central American States (ODECA) in 1951. In collaboration with the U.N. Economic Commission for Latin America, they had been moving since 1952 toward a plan for economic integration of the Central American states, which culminated in June 1958 with a treaty that laid the foundation for a Central American Common Market (CACM). The Treaty of Managua in December 1960, ratified by Guatemala in 1961, established the framework of the CACM, which brought a modest expansion of trade among the Central American states and fostered the expansion of manufacturing and food processing industries in Guatemala. The 1969 Honduras-El Salvador "Soccer War" set the integration movement back substantially when Honduras virtually withdrew. The CACM never fully lived up to its expectations, but it was a step toward economic integration of the five Central American states and Panama. The Secretariat for the Central American integration movement (SIECA) had its headquarters in Guatemala City. Guatemala's decision to impose many restrictions on trade in 1983 further weakened Central American integration as did the civil strife throughout the region in the 1980s.

Leading the 1963 coup against Ydígoras's was his Minister of Defense, Colonel Enrique Peralta Azurdia, who immediately declared a state of siege and established a military dictatorship. Specially trained troops accompanied by United States advisers checked the insurgents, although they could not suppress them entirely. Political leftists suffered assassination, arrest, or exile.

Victor Manuel Gutiérrez reportedly was dropped from an airplane 20,000 feet over the Pacific. Mario Méndez Montenengro, leader of the Revolutionary Party (PR), legal successor to Arévalo's PAR, was shot to death in 1965. Assassinations of other political activists, journalists, and labor leaders intimidated many more and maintained a reign of terror. The return of Jorge Ubico's remains from Louisiana for a state funeral in Guatemala symbolically reflected the return to the pre-1945 ideology that now dominated the government.

Under this sort of imposed stability and order, Peralta permitted free elections in 1966. The PR candidate, Julio César Méndez Montenegro, brother of the murdered leader of the party, won and took office. There was hope of a return to progressivism, but while the Army permitted Méndez to remain in the presidency, it did not allow him to rule. Some men would have resigned, as the Army was the real master of the country and continued the repression. Courageously, Méndez chose to make the best of a bad situation. He found he could achieve little of his program, however, and by the end of his term critics accused him of being a puppet of the military and a traitor to his brother's memory. The right-wing military took no chances in 1970, and, in an election that excluded most leftists, Colonel Carlos Arana Osorio won. In 1974 the military continued its disregard for free and open elections. Amid widespread cries of fraud, General Kjell Laugerud García, the son of a Norwegian immigrant, became President. Arana and Laugerud maintained peace and order with police-state efficiency. Business boomed, however, and the growing middle class enjoyed affluence despite debilitating inflation. The military elite began to enter the economy itself in a major way. Not only did the generals receive enormous salaries when they served as President, but they were able to use their positions to acquire private companies, large land holdings, and monopolistic concessions, amassing fortunes in the process. These Army officers established their own bank as a further institutional base for their economic interests. The corruption associated with this economic expansion and the wealth of these military officers reached obscene proportions in a country beset with staggering poverty among the majority of its population. An earthquake that killed more than 25,000 and devastated much of central Guatemala in February 1976 added to the misery.

The civil war continued, meanwhile, especially in the rugged, northern parts of the country where a limited road network made it more difficult for the Army to carry out operations. Political assassinations, "disappearances," and kidnappings on both sides were frequent in this "dirty war." By 1975 the FAR had suffered serious setbacks at the hands of the U.S.-supported counterinsurgency forces, but a new rebel force, calling itself the Guerrilla Army of the Poor (EGP), emerged in the northern Department of Quiché to continue the struggle. The FAR eventually reorganized and resumed active warfare in 1978.

In that same year General Romeo Lucas García of the Democratic Institutional Party (PID) succeeded to the presidency in a patently fraudulent election marred by widespread voter abstention. Guatemala's economic problems during this period were somewhat less serious than those of other Central American states because of the development of small but significant petroleum resources in the Petén and considerably less attention by the government to social welfare, but falling coffee, cotton, and sugar prices and the worldwide recession still had ill effects. Guatemala's trade deficit rose from $63 million in 1980 to $409 million by 1981. Lucas and right-wing death squads launched a brutal genocide against Indians suspected of supporting or joining the guerrillas. As the generals continued to seize large tracts of land, many indigenous people fled into Chiapas. Their numbers, in 149 refugee camps, had reached 180,000 by 1984. Activities of the clergy and international human rights organizations against the political oppression focused unfavorable attention on the country and damaged the tourist industry, which had become an important source of foreign exchange for Guatemala. Yet U.S. President Jimmy Carter's human rights policies had only hardened the resolve of the Guatemalan military and their death squads to deal violently with even moderate progressives such as the Christian Democrats (DCG). Guatemala simply replaced a partial cut-off of U.S. arms sales with arms and advisers from Israel until, under the presidency of Ronald Reagan, the U.S. resumed its military sales to Guatemala. Terror and assassination took a horrifying toll among leaders of labor organizations and at the University of San Carlos. In 1980 the civilian vice president, Francisco Villagrán Kramer, resigned in protest over the continued human rights violations.

Dissension within the military itself following the rigged election of another PID general, Ángel Aníbal Guevara. Younger officers supported by elements in both the right-wing MLN Party and the Christian Democrats moved to prevent his inauguration in March 1982, ousting Lucas during the last days of his regime in favor of a junta headed by retired General Efraín Ríos Montt. Ríos Montt, who assumed the presidency on 9 June, had been President Arana's Army Chief of Staff (1970–1974), but he also had been the presidential candidate of a coalition of parties headed by the Christian Democrats that had unsuccessfully claimed victory in 1974. Even more striking was his role as a minister of the California-based evangelical Christian Church of the Word. Evangelical Protestantism in Guatemala, with U.S. missionary support, grew remarkably after about 1960, to the extent that more than a quarter of Guatemala's population claimed Protestant affiliation. In contrast to the new Catholic evangelism in the country, which was associated with "liberation theology" and the political left, most of the Protestants were staunchly conservative and identified with pro-U.S. policies. In time, the Catholic missions began to restore Roman Catholic influence, especially during the papacy of John XXIII. The progressive attitude of some foreign Catholic missionaries—Maryknollers and Jesuits, for example, in the 1960s—created friction with the local, more traditional clergy. In the 1960s, too, the Church began to play a greater role in higher education, and it was notably important in organizing the Jesuit University of Rafael Landívar in Guatemala City in 1961.

Ríos Montt's accession to power changed the pattern of military rule. Superficially, at least, he made a noticeable effort to curb the corruption and to encourage higher ethical standards in the conduct of government. More impressive was the decline of death-squad activities and the restoration of security and peace in the central highlands, although Ríos Montt's hard-line policies with criminals drew the censure of human rights advocates. Political assassinations virtually ceased, and the disastrous decline of tourism, to which the violence had contributed, was reversed. Yet the economic and military power of the powerful generals who had ruled the country since 1954 could not be turned back, nor was Ríos Montt in any sense sympathetic to leftist interests. He, and the officers he represented, were principally concerned with preserving the privileged position of the military, and they believed that military abuses and corruption threatened the institution. Moreover, massacres of Indian communities continued, as did the flow of refugees into Mexico. He implemented a system of civil patrols inaugurated by the Lucas García administration, requiring Indians to serve, usually without firearms, as guardians against the guerrillas. Those who refused to serve received death sentences. Ríos Montt also suspended the Constitution, restricted labor unions, and prohibited the functioning of political parties in his effort to maintain order. In the meantime, the leftists united in January 1982 into the Guatemalan National Revolutionary Union (URNG), an umbrella organization for the PGT, FAR, EGP, and ORPA (Organization of the People in Arms, commanded by Rodrigo Asturias, son of the Nobel laureate, Miguel Ángel Asturias).

Ríos Montt's challenge to the military elite, his constant moralistic preaching, the excessively large role of U.S. Protestants in his advisory councils, imposition of a sales tax (IVA), and his meddling with powerful economic interests ensured that his regime was short-lived. On 8 August 1983, a new coup replaced him with Defense Minister General Oscar Humberto Mejía Victores. Whatever his motives, Ríos Montt's brief tenure as President of Guatemala began a process toward more democratic, civilian rule, and eventually the end of Guatemala's long civil war. Assessing the serious economic difficulties facing the country caused by falling coffee prices and declining tourism, as well as strong domestic and international censure of military atrocities in Guatemala, the military leaders decided to turn over limited power to civilians through relatively free elections in 1984 and 1985. Recent successful challenges to military dominance in Nicaragua and El Salvador undoubtedly influenced their thinking. In the meantime, a return to the high degree of corruption mentioned earlier, efforts to check the guerrillas who were now largely confined to the Petén, and failure to do anything about the growing poverty and economic problems facing the majority of the population characterized Mejía's government. Cynicism and anti-Communism were its most conspicuous qualities, with commitment to the same Neo-Liberal policies on behalf of the established elites that had characterized Guatemalan governments since 1954.

Elections for a Constitutional Assembly to write a new Constitution on 1 July 1984 reflected widespread voter apathy in the political process, in which seventeen parties (nine of them new) vied for the 88 seats. Mejía warned that the Assembly was limited strictly to writing a new constitution and electoral and *habeas corpus* laws. Moderates led the polling with the Christian Democratic (DCG) and National Centrist Union (UCN) parties winning a plurality, but with a coalition of diverse right-wing parties able to form a majority coalition. In reality, though, divisions among themselves prevented them from dominating the Assembly. The new Constitution, ratified on 31 May 1985, laid a foundation for the freest presidential election in Guatemala since 1945, won by the Christian Democrat Marco Vinicio Cerezo in December 1985.

Income Distribution in Guatemala, 1981

Percent of Population	*Monthly Income (US$)*
51.3	Less than $150
27.6	$151 to $300
8.4	$301 to $400
5.9	$401 to $600
3.5	$601 to $900
1.0	$901 to $1,200
1.3	More than $1,200

Source: Inforpress Centroamericano, *Centroamérica 1982, análisis económicos y políticos sobre la región* (Guatemala, 1982), p. 131.

9

Contemporary Guatemala

Rigoberta Menchú

Taking office in January 1986, Vinicio Cerezo quickly gave Guatemala's government a new tone. Although he was unable to end quickly the civil war and its accompanying human rights abuses, nor to suppress a rising narcotics trade, Cerezo promoted the Central American Peace Accord of 1987, which eventually brought a settlement to civil wars not only in Guatemala, but also in Nicaragua and El Salvador. In this effort Cerezo collaborated closely with Costa Rican President Oscar Arias.

The restoration of civilian rule in Guatemala did not immediately end the powerful influence of the high-ranking Guatemalan Army officers. It became clear early in Cerezo's administration that his authority was at their pleasure. Military violations of human rights continued to plague Guatemala, the continued resistance of leftist rebels providing a justification for repressive action in the eyes of the military. The U.S. had again cut off military aid to Guatemala in 1990, but this did not deter the military from shielding their own from prosecution for civil rights violations. It was the compassionate voice of an indigenous K'iche' woman, Rigoberta Menchú, however, that brought the plight of the Guatemalan people to worldwide attention, increasing international pressure on the Guatemalan government to end the conflict by negotiating with the rebels. Menchú received the 1992 Nobel Peace Prize, "in recognition of her work for social justice and ethno-cultural reconciliation based on respect for the rights of indigenous peoples." Traditional Guatemalan elites, including Cerezo's successor, President Jorge Serrano, belittled the award.

The rising popularity of General Efraín Ríos Montt resulted in remarkable realignments in the Guatemalan political spectrum during the campaign for Cerezo's successor. With the leftist parties still outlawed in 1990, a large number of parties from extreme right to center vied for the presidency. The new Constitution prohibited from candidacy anyone who had participated in an attempt to overthrow the government, a provision challenged by Ríos Montt, but the courts eventually disqualified him late in the campaign. Cerezo's Christian Democrats had become strong in the 1980s, but the continued civil war, economic uncertainty, and charges of widespread corruption heavily discredited the DCG. Moreover, the more open political climate had allowed peasant and labor organizations to become more vocal in their demands, but little tangible benefits came their way, causing widespread disenchantment with his government. The owner of an important Guatemala City daily newspaper, *El Gráfico*, Jorge Carpio Nicolle of the National Centrist Union (UCN) was the leading challenger to the DCG, but Carpio failed to win the presidency in both 1985 and 1990, although his party remained important in the Congress in the early 1990s. As it turned out, Ríos Montt's disqualification late in the campaign paved the way for the meteoric rise of Jorge Serrano Elías's Solidarity Action Movement (MAS). Serrano was a right-wing engineer and businessman, but also an evangelical Protestant closely allied with Ríos Montt. He not only picked up much of the large vote that would have gone to Ríos Montt, but also captured the imagination of many urban Guatemalans disenchanted with both Carpio and the DCG's lackluster candidate, Alfonso Cabrera. In the 11 November 1990, election, in which left-wing parties urged voters to boycott the polls, Carpio led the polling with 27.5 percent, followed by Serrano's 24.2 percent, and Cabrera's 17.5 percent. Álvaro Arzú Irigoyen, former Mayor of Guatemala and successful head of the National Tourism Board, at the head of the Neo-Liberal National Advancement Party (PAN), placed a close fourth with 17.3 percent. Eight other candidates trailed far behind. Significantly, voter abstention, which had dropped to 26 percent in the 1985 elections, soared to 51 percent, reflecting either voter disenchantment or commitment to Ríos Montt. The PAN, although failing to win the presidency, won the mayorship of Guatemala City and a large number of seats in the legislature.

Serrano appeared to be skillful at political dealing when he gained the endorsements of Cerezo and of Arzú. In the run-off election on 6 January 1991, Serrano whipped Carpio with an impressive 68.7 percent of the vote and carried 21 of Guatemala's 22 departments. On the next day he designated Arzú as his Foreign Minister. Other PAN members also received appointment to high offices.

Although Serrano advanced the cause of a peace settlement with the guerrillas and promised more rapid economic development, political violence continued during his administration, and his lack of political experience became quickly evident. An earthquake shook the country in September 1991, killing 53 and leaving 30,000 homeless, adding to the socioeconomic problems, especially of the poor. In May 1993, apparently frustrated by his inability to control the military or to check the rising opposition of labor and other opposition mass organizations, Serrano seized dictatorial control, in what some called a "self-coup," as he disbanded the Congress and all political parties. This move, apparently approved by the Army, met massive popular protests. Then, when the traditionally docile legislature refused to disband and instead demanded his resignation, the Army backed down, forcing Serrano's resignation on 1 June 1993. The Congress promptly elected Ramiro de León Carpio, the Human Rights Ombudsman, as interim president. The Army accepted this, but rejected the new president's choice for Defense Minister, emphasizing its right to choose that official. Although de León Carpio brought about some reforms aimed at a reduction in government corruption, it was evident once more that the military still held ultimate authority in Guatemala. Soon thereafter the assassination of his cousin, UCN leader Jorge Carpio Nicolle along with three of his associates, in an ambush near Chichicastenango, highlighted the reality that there was still much instability in the country. Carpio had written strong editorials opposing a general amnesty designed to pardon all those involved in Serrano's self-coup. The military was suspected in his assassination and an arrest was made, but no one was ever convicted in a case that emphasized the impotence of the government against the military.

Political alignments continued to shift in the 1990s, as the multitude of parties coalesced into working coalitions. The DCG and UCN had shrunk to minor party status by 1995. In that year they joined with the Social Democratic Party (PSD), to form the Alianza Nacional, which won only four seats in the Congress. Álvaro Arzú's PAN, meanwhile, gained the support of several center-right parties to form a congressional majority in 1995. More extreme right-wing interests followed Ríos Montt's leadership of the Guatemalan Republican Front (FRG). After this party's victories in congressional elections, Ríos Montt became President of the Guatemalan Congress in January 1995 and immediately launched a new bid for the presidency. Once again the courts upheld the constitutional prohibition of his candidacy. In his place, Alfonso Portillo headed the FRG ticket. In the November 1995 election, Arzú and Portillo led the polling with 37 and 22 percent respectively, with the Alianza Nacional receiving only 13 percent, and a new leftist coalition, the New Guatemala Democratic Front (FDNG) receiving 8 percent. Again, abstention ran high, with only 47 percent of registered voters participating. In the runoff on 7 January Arzú, with 51.2 percent of the vote, won a narrow victory over Portillo's 48.7 percent. Abstention was even greater than in the November election, with only about a third of registered voters participating. Arzú's victory reflected his strength in the capital, however, for Portillo carried most of the countryside and 18 of Guatemala's 22 departments.

Arzú took office in January 1996 and pursued a strongly Neo-Liberal agenda, with establishment of peace with the guerrillas a top priority of his administration. The rebels had essentially lost the military struggle by this time and following a series of agreements concluded in Oslo, Mexico, and Madrid, they signed a formal peace accord in Guatemala City on 29 December 1996. It allowed the guerrillas to return to peaceful political life in Guatemala. The formal end of the 36-year civil war that had killed more than 100,000 Guatemalans was a major event, although the details of its implementation dragged on throughout 1997. An estimated 40,000 more had "disappeared" and up to a million had been forced from their homes or into exile. The former guerrillas and other outlawed leftist parties now joined the FDNG.

Arzú made significant progress in reducing human rights abuses. He dismissed military officers accused of human rights violations. This purge left behind military officers who accepted, or at least did not actively oppose, the UN-mediated peace talks with the guerrillas. Yet the 1998 assassination of Bishop Juan Gerardi Conedera, who had documented in detail the atrocities that had been committed during the 36-year civil war and the failure of the government to stem the continuing violence, revealed the depth of the problem. Intimidation of judges and prosecutors in the Gerardi cases brought their resignations and the case remained unsolved. A wave of kidnappings and other criminal acts followed amid a generally rising crime rate in the country as the Neo-Liberal economic policies followed in recent years improved many economic indicators, but failed to reverse the trend toward declining standards of living for most Guatemalans. Although a significant, if small, middle class had emerged in Guatemala, the vast majority of the populace remained poor. A survey in 1999 revealed that 88 percent of Guatemalans felt that the administration of justice was inadequate. A UN-sponsored report called Guatemala City the most dangerous city in the Americas.

Guatemala continued to claim Belize (formerly British Honduras), but found herself increasingly isolated as other Latin American states declared support for the independence of that tiny enclave of British colonialism on Guatemala's Caribbean shore. Belize's economic decline of the late nineteenth century had continued, and the colony was more of a liability than an asset to Great Britain. It produced a few bananas and some sugar for export, and there was some improvement in the mahogany market, but chicle and citrus fruit became its principal exports. Growing and smuggling of marijuana and other illegal substances was also on the rise. Except for a small section of the town where the foreign company and diplomatic representatives lived alongside a tiny local elite, Belize City remained an unsavory, tropical village, with unpainted wooden houses, dirty streets, and open sewers.

After World War II economic pressures forced the devaluation of the British Honduras dollar and the economic difficulties that followed led to the first serious challenge to the status quo when George Price formed the People's United Party (PUP). Labor struggles of the 1930s had begun the process of more active black participation in Belizean politics, but it was Price who mobilized diverse elements of the population into an effective political force. Price, educated in the United States, had served as secretary for local multimillionaire Robert Sidney Turton. His leftist party gained wide support from working people. Because it was anti-British, PUP also received support from the Arbenz government in neighboring Guatemala, which hoped to win PUP support of Guatemalan sovereignty over Belize.

In 1954 the PUP won control of the Belize legislature. Although the party split over the question of friendship with Guatemala, it soundly defeated the newly-formed Honduras Independence Party (HIP), which favored entry into the West Indian Federation. Price, as Prime Minister, directed modest economic improvements and moved the colony closer to independence, winning reelection in 1961. Soon thereafter, Hurricane Hattie swept over Belize City, its tidal surge and winds causing massive destruction. This event led directly to the decision to establish a new capital inland at a place to be named Belmopan. The new public buildings, inspired by Maya architecture, somehow fell short of Maya grandeur. The new capital grew very slowly and Belize City continued for many years to be the site of much of the government's operations, even after Belize became self-governing in 1963 and gradually moved toward full independence. By 1995 Belmopan still had only about 5,000 residents, but grew to more than 12,000 by 2005, when the entire country had only about 283,000 people, of which 85,000 lived in Belize City. An expanding tourist trade, capitalizing on the excellent fishing and scuba diving along Belize's coral reef, and new agricultural development by North American enterprises had by then triggered some economic growth and diversification.

Guatemala severed diplomatic relations with Panama over the latter's support for Belizean independence in 1977, but soon after several other Latin American states also declared their support for Belize and in November the United Nations General Assembly adopted a resolution favoring independence by a vote of 126-4 (with 13 abstentions). The U.S. had generally followed a slightly pro-Guatemalan neutrality in the dispute, but in November 1980 it supported another UN resolution (passed 139-0, with 7 abstentions) calling for Belizean independence. This resolution called on Britain to continue to defend Belize and later received endorsement from the Organization of American States (OAS), which until then had officially supported Guatemala's claim. Guatemala repeatedly threatened to attack Belize, but also entered long-term negotiations to resolve the dispute and in March 1981 begrudgingly agreed to accept Belizean independence, aware that British troops guaranteed its territorial integrity. Subsequent talks soon collapsed, however, and Guatemala once more broke relations with Britain and closed her Belizean consulates. On 21 September 1981 Belize officially became an independent constitutional monarchy within the British Commonwealth and soon thereafter joined the OAS.

President Cerezo initiated new negotiations with Belize, and in 1991 the Serrano government officially recognized Belizean independence. Subsequently, the Guatemalan Court of Constitutionality and the Guatemalan Congress confirmed that action. But after Serrano's fall, new Guatemalan challenges to this policy led the Congress to reverse itself and to brand Serrano a traitor for acting without prior approval from the legislature. Since then Guatemala has sought a solution that would cede a portion of southern Belize to Guatemala. Various border incidents repeatedly inflamed relations between the two states. A Guatemalan commission visited Belize in 1997 in a new effort to resolve the matter but these talks ended in failure. The British government at one point offered to pay Guatemala US$24 million in return for dropping its claim to Belize. Military officers from Guatemala and Belize met in July 2000 in an effort to reduce tension along their border. The OAS negotiated a temporary agreement, signed in 2003, to end the dispute, but Guatemalan voters rejected the proposed treaty and it was never brought to a vote in Belize. Continuing discussions under OAS auspices have failed to achieve a permanent settlement of the dispute through 2005, but the issue now appears to be quietly fading.

Belizean independence accelerated popular demands for more equitable land and income distribution. A modest land reform program begun in 1962 had distributed more than a half-million acres to small farmers by 1982, but since that date large-scale agroexport agriculture has become dominant, as Belize shifted from a forestry economy to one based on citrus and other agroexports. United States economic influence largely supplanted the British during the twentieth century. There was a notable increase in seafood exports. But, as with much of the rest of Central America in the 1990s, imports rose more rapidly than exports. Belize's balance of trade deficit thus soared from US$56 million in 1975 to $328 million by 2004. Emphasis on economic development by the PUP tended to divert its focus from working class issues. More radical groups such as UBAD (United Black Association for Development), PAC (People's Action Committee) and RAM (Revolitical Action Movement) increasingly challenged the PUP's middle-class orientation. UBAD began in 1969 as a black nationalist organization and then evolved into a major political party after independence. It pressured the PUP to devote more attention to education at all levels and to improvement in wage levels. The leftist groups eroded the constituency of the PUP, which in 1984 led to victory by the more conservative United Democratic Party (UDP). Price returned to power in 1989, but when he called for new elections in mid-1993, 15 months before they were scheduled, he lost his premiership in a close election to the UDP's Manuel Esquivel. Esquivel led the country along the Neo-Liberal policies being pursued by all the Central American states in the 1990s, but by 1997 the new PUP leader, Said Musa, was regaining support for the PUP with his charges that these policies had resulted in increased poverty, unemployment, high inflation, rising crime, and a slow-down in economic growth. In 1998 Musa became Prime Minister and the PUP again won elections in 2003 allowing him to continue in that office to the present (2005). Increased tourism more recently has bolstered the Belizean economy with economic growth running well ahead of inflation. Hurricanes sometimes caused serious damage, however, and by 2005 the government still classified a third of the population as living in poverty, with unemployment at around 12 percent.

Meanwhile, the 1990s witnessed a rejuvenation of the Central American Common Market and establishment of a new Central American Free Trade Zone by 1993. Tariffs gradually fell and there was substantial growth again in trade between Guatemala and the other Central American states. Increasingly, however, the Guatemalan Neo-Liberals focused on expanding free trade agreements with Mexico, the United States, and Canada. The United States remained by far the principal source of Guatemalan imports and destination of Guatemalan exports. Guatemala and the United States ratified a Central American Free Trade Agreement (CAFTA) in 2005, over widespread opposition and violent protests from Guatemalan workers.

As Guatemala began the twenty-first century violence and human rights abuses still haunted the country. Indigenous Guatemalans, however, had notably increased their representation in the government and had formed their own political party, the National Civic Political Forum of Maya Unity and Fraternity, in February 1999. Still, they held only six of eighty seats in the Guatemalan Congress while constituting more than 60 percent of Guatemala's population. Control of the country continued to rest with the descendants of the creole elite and foreign investors, but it had become a much larger and more complex upper class.

In the presidential election of 1999, Alfonso Portillo (FRG), with Ríos Montt's backing, defeated Guatemala City Mayor, Oscar Berger (PAN), winning 68 percent of the vote in the 26 December runoff and taking office in January 2000. Violence continued to limit Guatemala's economic growth. Rigoberta Menchú led human rights organizations to file a class-action suit before Spanish courts against Ríos Montt and seven other Guatemalan military and civil officials for alleged crimes relating to the 1980 burning of the Spanish Embassy in Guatemala in which

39 Guatemalans had died. Charges were also filed in Guatemalan courts against three military officials who were finally arrested for the 1998 assassination of Bishop Gerardi, although more recently doubt has arisen as to their actual guilt. The violence caused many to leave the country, especially poor people who were fleeing to Mexico and the United States. Their remittances to friends and relatives remaining in Guatemala has come to be a major source of foreign exchange in the country, second only to revenues from coffee exports. Meanwhile, Guatemala was becoming a major producer and clandestine exporter to the United States of illegal drugs. The U.S. Drug Enforcement Agency repeatedly charged that Guatemala was a transshipment point for Colombian cocaine and heroin. This led to an agreement in 2000 with the United States for U.S. military and special agents to begin operations within Guatemala against the drug interests.

Scandals involving corruption eroded support for Portillo throughout his four-year term. A legislative inquiry in 2001, known as "Guategate" resulted in 24 indictments, including one against the President of the Congress, Ríos Montt. Although the courts exonerated Ríos Montt, the controversy continued along with other charges of government corruption, financial mismanagement, and conflict of interest. Portillo's frequent trips abroad and the high crime rate were further sources of criticism. Despite widespread rumors of an impending *coup d'état*, however, Portillo managed to complete his term. Attention to his problems were at least temporarily diverted by a visit to Guatemala by Pope John Paul II in late July 2002 and by his canonization of Brother Pedro de San José de Betancurt on 30 July 2002, the only Central American ever to achieve sainthood.

By 2003 Portillo and the FRG had little remaining popular support. As early as 2002 a *Vox Latina* poll had reported that only eight percent of Guatemalans had any confidence in the President and 41 percent regarded him as the worst president in Guatemalan history. Guatemala's refusal to support the U.S.-led war in Iraq garnered Portillo considerable popular support on that issue, but also contributed to a cooling of relations with the U.S. In July of 2003 the Court of Constitutionality finally ruled that Ríos Montt could be a candidate for the presidency, but he was unable to overcome the falling reputation of the FRG and in the November elections he finished well behind Oscar Berger (of the rightist coalition Grand National Alliance) and Álvaro Colom (of the leftist coalition National Unity of Hope). In the December runoff, Berger won 54 percent to Colom's 46 percent and became President on 14 January 2004.

Berger pursued a clearly Neo-Liberal agenda that emphasized productivity and a pledge to increase employment. But he also sought to improve the lot of the indigenous peoples. He recognized former governments' responsibility for much of the country's violence when he ordered compensation to peasants for lands and lives lost during the long civil war (1961–1996). In other symbolic moves he turned over the Casa Crema—formerly the presidential palace and headquarters for the Army for the past 40 years—to the Academy of Mayan Languages and Maya TV, and then he named Rigoberta Menchú to take charge of the implementation of the 1996 Peace Accords. He also reduced the size of the Army, shifting some military personnel to the National Police in an effort to stem the continuing high rates of murder, violence against women, kidnappings, land conflicts, and violations of civil rights. The Berger government also took action against former high officials involved in corrupt practices. Berger openly praised a UN plan to appoint special prosecutors to investigate human rights abuses, but some military officers and other government officials managed to delay its implementation. The first military officer convicted of a war crime, Col. Juan Valencia Osorio, for the 1990 murder of sociologist Myrna Mack, went into hiding before he could be jailed. Then former President Portillo fled to Mexico after the Court of Constitutionality removed his immunity from prosecution. But General

Ríos Montt was placed under house arrest pending his trial for having organized a violent political riot during the last presidential campaign. Berger's actions on behalf of human rights led the U.S. government in 2005 to resume military aid to Guatemala.

Notwithstanding these problems, there were areas of improvement in the country. Coffee prices began to turn upward by 2005 and more diversified manufacturing and agricultural production contributed to both rising employment and increased economic activity. There was a notable improvement in public health, thanks especially to considerable aid from the Cuban government, which has equipped six new hospitals in Guatemala and sent some 200 physicians to work in them since 1998. Cuba has also provided scholarships for hundreds of Guatemalans to study medicine in Havana. Conditions for women notably improved in reproductive health and education. The infant mortality rate in Guatemala fell from 40 to 16 per 1,000 live births and the occurrences of many epidemic diseases was significantly reduced. Meanwhile, the beauty of the country continued to draw tourists who brought much needed foreign exchange to Guatemala. The Neo-Liberal economic policies of the government, while controversial, were moving Guatemala into the globalized economy, while the traditional dominance of the military in Guatemalan history appeared to be diminishing. Guatemala faced the challenges of the twenty-first century with grounds for optimism, but also with serious obstacles to progress.

Appendix

Chiefs of State of Guatemala Since 1524

Kings of Spain

Habsburgs:

1516–1556	Carlos I (Charles V of Holy Roman Empire (1519–1556))
1556–1598	Felipe II
1598–1621	Felipe III
1621–1665	Felipe IV
1665–1700	Carlos II

Bourbons:

1700–1746	Felipe V
1746–1759	Fernando VI
1759–1788	Carlos III
1788–1808	Carlos IV
1808–1814	Joseph Bonaparte (not recognized in Guatemala)
1814–1833	Fernando VII

Captains General and Governors Under the Spanish Empire

1524–1526	Pedro de Alvarado y Contreras
1526	Gonzalo de Alvarado y Contreras
1526–1527	Pedro de Portocarrero
1527–1529	Jorge de Alvarado
1529–1530	Agustín Francisco de Orduña

1530–1533	Pedro de Alvarado y Contreras
1533–1535	Jorge de Alvarado
1535–1536	Pedro de Alvarado y Contreras
1536–1539	Alonso de Maldonado de Paz
1539–1540	Pedro de Alvarado y Contreras
1540–1541	Francisco de la Cueva y Villacreces
1541	Beatriz de Alva de la Cueva de Alvarado
1541–1542	Francisco de la Cueva y Villacreces and Francisco Marroquín, governing jointly
1542–1548	Alonso de Maldonado de Paz
1548–1554	Alonso López Cerrato
1554–1558	Antonio Rodríguez de Quesada
1558–1559	Pedro Ramírez de Quiñónes
1559–1564	Juan Núñez de Landecho
1564–1570	Francisco Briceño
1570–1573	Antonio González
1573–1578	Pedro de Villalobos
1578–1589	Pedro García de Valverde
1589–1594	Pedro Mallén de Rueda
1594–1596	Francisco de Sande Picón
1596–1598	Álvaro Gómez de Abaunza
1598–1611	Alonso Criado de Castilla
1611–1627	Antonio Peraza Ayala Castilla y Rojas, Conde de La Gomera
1627–1634	Diego de Acuña
1634–1642	Álvaro de Quiñónes y Osorio y Miranda, Marqués de Lorenzana
1642–1649	Diego de Avendaño
1649–1654	Antonio de Lara y Mogrovejo (Acting Governor)
1654–1657	Fernando de Altamirano y Velasco, Conde de Santiago de Calimaya
1657–1659	The Audiencia directed the kingdom during this period

1659–1668	Martín Carlos de Mencos
1668–1670	Sebastián Álvarez Alonso Rosica de Caldas
1670–1672	Juan de Santa María Sáenz Mañosca y Murillo
1672–1678	Fernando Francisco de Escobedo
1678–1681	Lope de Sierra Osorio
1681–1683	Juan Miguel Augurto y Alava
1683–1688	Enrique Enríquez de Guzmán
1688–1691	Jacinto de Barrios y Leal
1691–1694	Fernando Lope de Ursino y Orbaneja
1694–1695	Jacinto de Barrios y Leal
1695–1696	José Scals
1696–1702	Gabriel Sánchez de Berrospe
1702–1703	Alonso de Ceballos y Villagutierre
1703–1706	Juan Jerónimo Duardo
1706–1716	Toribio José de Cosío y Campo, Marqués de Torre Campo
1716–1724	Francisco Rodríguez de Rivas
1724–1733	Pedro Antonio de Echévers y Subiza
1733–1742	Pedro Rivera y Villalón
1742–1748	Tomás Rivera y Santa Cruz
1748–1752	José Araujo y Río
1752–1753	José Vásquez Prego Montaos y Sotomayor
1753–1754	Juan de Velarde y Cienfuegos
1754–1760	Alonso de Arcos y Moreno
1760–1761	Juan de Velarde y Cienfuegos
1761–1765	Alonso de Fernández de Heredia
1765–1771	Pedro de Salazar y Herrera Nájera y Mendoza
1771–1773	Juan González Bustillo y Villaseñor
1773–1779	Martín de Mayorga
1779–1783	Matías de Gálvez García Madrid y Cabrera
1783–1789	José de Estachería
1789–1794	Bernardo Troncoso Martínez del Rincón
1794–1801	José Domás y Valle
1801–1811	Antonio González Mollinedo y Saravia

1811–1818	José de Bustamante y Guerra
1818–1821	Carlos de Urrutia y Montoya

CAPTAINS GENERAL AND
GOVERNORS UNDER THE MEXICAN EMPIRE

1821–1822	Gabino Gaínza
1822–1823	Vicente Filísola

CHIEF EXECUTIVES OF
THE UNITED PROVINCES OF CENTRAL AMERICA

1823–1825	A series of provisional juntas ruled the country until elections for president were held in 1825
1825–1828	Manuel José Arce
1828–1829	Mariano Beltranena
1829–1830	José Francisco Barrundia
1830–1838	Francisco Morazán
1839	Diego Vijil

GOVERNORS OF THE STATE OF GUATEMALA (UPCA)

1824–1826	Juan Barrundia
1826	Cirilio Flores
1827	José Domingo Estrada
1827–1829	Mariano de Aycinena y Piñol
1829	Juan Barrundia
1829–1830	Pedro Molina Mazariegos
1830–1831	Antonio Rivera Cabezas
1831–1838	Mariano Gálvez
1838–1841	Mariano Rivera Paz
1839	Carlos Salazar (temporarily)
1841–1842	José Venacio López (temporarily)
1842–1844	Mariano Rivera Paz
1844–1847	Gen. Rafael Carrera (except for September-November 1845 when he turned power over to Vice President Vicente Cruz)

Presidents of the Republic of Guatemala

1847–1848	Gen. Rafael Carrera
1848	Juan Antonio Martínez
1851–1865	Gen. Rafael Carrera
1865	Pedro de Aycinena
1865–1871	Field Marshall Vicente Cerna
1871–1873	Gen. Miguel García Granados
1873–1882	Gen. Justo Rufino Barrios
1882–1883	Gen. José María Orantes
1883–1885	Gen. Justo Rufino Barrios
1885	Alejandro M. Sinibaldi
1885–1892	Gen. Manuel Lisandro Barillas
1892–1898	Gen. José María Reina Barrios
1898–1920	Manuel Estrada Cabrera
1920–1921	Carlos Herrera
1921–1926	Gen. José María Orellana
1926–1930	Gen. Lázaro Chacón
1930	Baudilio Palma
1930–1931	Gen. Manuel Orellana
1931	José María Reina Andrade
1931–1944	Jorge Ubico Castañeda
1944	Gen. Federico Ponce Vaides
1944–1945	Junta Revolucionaria: Col. Jacobo Arbenz Guzmán, Jorge Toriello Garrido, Major Francisco Javier Arana
1945–1951	Juan José Arévalo Bermejo
1951–1954	Col. Jacobo Arbenz Guzmán
1954	Col. Carlos Enrique Díaz de León
1954	Military Junta: Col. Carlos Enrique Díaz, Col. José Ángel Sánchez, Col. Elfego H. Monzón
1954	Military Junta: Col. Elfego H. Monzón, Col. José Luis Salazar, Col. Mauricio Dubois
1954	Military Junta: Col. Elfego H. Monzón, Col. José Luis Salazar, Col. Mauricio Dubois, Col. Carlos Castillo Armas, Col. Enrique Trinidad Oliva

1954	Military Junta: Col. Enrique Trinidad Oliva, Col. Elfego H. Monzón, Col. Carlos Castillo Armas
1954–1957	Col. Carlos Castillo Armas
1957	Luis Arturo González López
1957	Military Junta: Col. Oscar Mendoza Azurdia, Col. Roberto Lorenzana Salazar, Col. Gonzalo Yurrita Nova
1957–1958	Col. Guillermo Flores Avendaño
1958–1963	Gen. Miguel Ydígoras Fuentes
1963–1966	Col. Enrique Peralta Azurdia
1966–1970	Julio César Méndez Montenegro
1970–1974	Gen. Carlos Manuel Arana Osorio
1974–1978	Gen. Kjell Eugenio Laugerud García
1978–1982	Gen. Fernando Romeo Lucas García
1982–1983	Gen. Efraín Ríos Montt
1983–1986	Gen. Oscar Humberto Mejía Victores
1986–1992	Marco Vinicio Cerezo Arévalo
1992–1993	Jorge Antonio Serrano Elías
1993–1996	Ramiro de León Carpio
1996–2000	Álvaro Enrique Arzú Irigoyen
2000–2004	Alfonso Antonio Portillo Cabrera
2004–	Oscar Berger Perdomo

Sources: David Henige, *Colonial Governors from the Fifteenth Century to the Present* (Madison: University of Wisconsin Press, 1970); Francis Polo Sifontes, *Nuestros gobernantes (1821–1981)* (Guatemala: Editorial "José de Pineda Ibarra", 1981); J. Antonio Villacorta C., *Historia de la Capitanía General de Guatemala* (Guatemala: Tipografía Nacional, 1942); Richard E. Moore, *Historical Dictionary of Guatemala* (Metuchen, N.J.: Scarecrow Press, 1967); Ernesto Bienvenido Jiménez, *Ellos los presidentes* (Guatemala: Editorial "José Pineda Ibarra", 1981); and Alejandro Marure, *Efemérides de los hechos notables acaecidos en la República de Centro América, desde el año de 1821 hasta el de 1842, seguidas de varios catálogos de presidentes de la República, jefes de estado, etc.* (Guatemala: Tipografía Nacional, 1895).

Glossary of Terms Used

alcalde – mayor, or chief officer of an ayuntamiento

alcaldes mayores – chief officers at the county, or Alcaldía Mayor level

audiencia – supreme court, exercising judicial, legislative, and executive authority in the colonial Kingdom of Guatemala

ayuntamiento – city council

caciques – indigenous chiefs, recognized by the Spaniards and sometimes coopted

caudillo – charismatic political chief who rules with a strong hand

colonos – workers residing permanently on a landed estate required to work for the owner

consulado de comercio – merchant guild

corregidor – colonial Spanish official in charge of a district called a *corregimiento*. The position was similar to the alcalde mayor, who oversaw an alcaldía mayor. Both can be compared in size and function to a U.S. county.

creole – a person of Spanish descent born in the New World

encomienda – a grant of the labor and tribute of indigenous people given to a Spanish settler (*encomendero*) by the Spanish crown. In return for being allowed the use these native laborers, the encomenderos were required to insure that they were Christianized. Important in the sixteenth century, the institution gradually was replaced by the *repartimiento* (*q.v.*) in the seventeenth century.

finca – a farm or plantation

fuero – of medieval origin, in Spanish law a fuero granted rights to a specific group or class, giving them exclusive privileges and protections, including their own courts of law, meeting places, and immunity from certain laws or practices. Such fueros were held, for example, by the military, clergy, merchants, lawyers, physicians, etc.

jornaleros – workers employed by the day or for specific periods

junta – a small group of persons organized for a specific purpose, as a commission, but often a group of military officers, sometimes including civilians, to temporarily rule a country

ladino – mixture of European and indigenous ethnicity, in practice including indigenous peoples who adopted Spanish language and customs

mandamiento – a system of forced wage labor

oidores – justices of the Audiencia, or Supreme Court

peninsular – a person born on the Iberian peninsula

positivism – the materialistic theory, popular in late nineteenth-century Latin America, that science is the only valid source of knowledge. Based heavily on the ideas of Auguste Comte, of France, it emphasized order and progress and was popular in Guatemala among those who favored economic development. It was sometimes used to justify strong central government.

procuradores – lobbyists, or representatives of special interest or outlying provinces to push for their interests at the royal court

repartimiento – a forced labor system that granted labor of indigenous communities to Spanish or creole settlers, government agencies, or the Church in colonial Guatemala

residencia – a formal investigation carried out at the conclusion of a government official's term of office in colonial Spanish America

zambos – people of mixed indigenous and African ethnicity

Suggestions for Additional Reading in English

General Works and Works of Broad Utility

Handy, Jim. *Gift of the Devil: A History of Guatemala.* Boston: South End Press, 1984.

Holden, Robert. *Armies Without Nations: Public Violence and State Formation in Central America.* New York: Oxford University Press, 2004.

McCreery, David J. *Rural Guatemala, 1760–1940.* Stanford, California: Stanford University Press, 1994.

Pérez Brignoli, Héctor. *A Brief History of Central America.* Berkeley: University of California Press, 1989.

Robinson, William I. *Transnational Conflicts: Central America, Social Change, and Globalization.* London: Verso, 2003.

Smith, Carol A., ed. *Guatemalan Indians and the State, 1540–1988.* Austin: University of Texas Press, 1990.

Tenenbaum, Barbara A., ed. *Encyclopedia of Latin American History and Culture*, 5 vols. New York: Charles Scribner's Sons, 1996.

Woodward, Jr., Ralph Lee. *Central America: A Nation Divided*, 3rd ed. New York: Oxford University Press, 1999.

Chapter 1: The Land of the Maya

Carmack, Robert M. *The Quiché Mayas of Utatlán: The Evolution of a Highland Guatemala Kingdom.* Norman: University of Oklahoma Press, 1981.

Coe, Michael D. *Breaking the Maya Code*, rev. ed. New York: Thames and Hudson, 1999.

———. *The Maya*, 7th ed. London and New York: Thames and Hudson, 2005.

Demarest, Arthur, Prudence Rice, and Don Rice, eds. *The Terminal Classic in the Maya Lowlands.* Boulder: University Press of Colorado, 2004.

Diamond, Jared. *Collapse: How Societies Choose to Fail or Succeed.* New York: Viking, 2005.

Fischer, Edward F. *Cultural Logics and Global Economies: Maya Identity in Thought and Practice.* Austin: University of Texas Press, 2001.

Hunter, C. Bruce. *A Guide to Ancient Maya Ruins*, rev. ed. Norman: University of Oklahoma Press, 1986.

Sabloff, Jeremy. *The New Archaeology and the Ancient Maya.* New York: Scientific American Library, 1990.

Sharer, Robert. *The Ancient Maya.* Stanford, Califorina: Stanford University Press, 1994.

Webster, David. *The Fall of the Ancient Maya.* New York: Thames & Hudson, 2002.

Chapter 2: Europeanization

Few, Martha. *Women Who Live Evil Lives: Gender, Religion, and the Politics of Power in Colonial Guatemala.* Austin: University of Texas Press, 2002.

Herrera, Robinson A. *Natives, Europeans, and Africans in Sixteenth-Century Santiago de Guatemala.* Austin: University of Texas Press, 2003.

Lovell, W. George. *Conquest and Survival in Colonial Guatemala: A Historical Geography of the Cuchumatán Highlands, 1500–1821,* 3rd ed. Kingston & Montreal: McGill-Queen's University Press, 2004.

Lutz, Christopher. *Santiago de Guatemala, 1541–1773: City, Caste, and the Colonial Experience.* Norman: University of Oklahoma Press, 1994.

MacLeod, Murdo. *Spanish Central America: A Socioeconomic History, 1520–1720.* Berkeley: University of California Press, 1973.

Chapter 3: Independence

Brown, Richmond F. *Juan Fermín de Aycinena, Central American Colonial Entrepreneur, 1729–1796.* Norman: University of Oklahoma Press, 1997.

Hawkins, Timothy. *José de Bustamante and Central American Independence: Colonial Administration in an Age of Imperial Crisis.* Tuscaloosa: University of Alabama Press, 2004.

Lanning, John Tate. *The Eighteenth-Century Enlightenment in the University of San Carlos de Guatemala.* Ithaca: New York, Cornell University Press, 1956.

———. *The University in the Kingdom of Guatemala.* Ithaca: New York, Cornell University Press, 1955.

Patch, Robert W. *Maya Revolt and Revolution in the Eighteenth Century.* London: M. E. Sharpe, 2002.

Wortman, Miles. *Government and Society in Central America, 1680–1840.* New York: Columbia University Press, 1982.

CHAPTER 4: THE UNITED PROVINCES OF CENTRAL AMERICA

Hawkins, Timothy. "War of Words: Manuel Montúfar, Alejandro Marure, and the Politics of History in Guatemala," *The Historian* 64 (Spring/Summer 2002): 513–533.

Karnes, Thomas L. *The Failure of Union: Central America, 1824–1975*, rev. ed. Tempe: Center for Latin American Studies, Arizona State University, 1976.

Rodríguez, Mario. *The Cádiz Experiment in Central America, 1808–1826.* Berkeley: University of California Press, 1978.

CHAPTER 5: THE REPUBLIC OF GUATEMALA

Griffith, William J. *Empires in the Wilderness: Foreign Colonization and Development in Guatemala, 1834–1844.* Chapel Hill: University of North Carolina Press, 1966.

Rodriguez, Mario. *A Palmerstonian Diplomat in Central America: Frederick Chatfield, Esq.* Tucson: University of Arizona Press, 1964.

Pattridge, Blake D. *Institution Building and State Formation in Nineteenth-Century Latin America: The University of San Carlos, Guatemala.* New York: Peter Lang, 2004.

Sullivan-González, Douglass. *Piety, Power, and Politics: Religion and Nation Formation in Guatemala, 1821–1871*. Pittsburgh: University of Pittsburgh Press, 1998.

Woodward, Jr., Ralph Lee. *Rafael Carrera and the Emergence of the Republic of Guatemala, 1821–1871*. Athens: University of Georgia Press, 1993.

Chapter 6: Liberal Guatemala

Dosal, Paul J. *Doing Business with the Dictators: A Political History of United Fruit in Guatemala, 1899–1944*. Wilmington, Delaware: Scholarly Resources, 1993.

Grieb, Kenneth. *Guatemalan Caudillo: The Regime of Jorge Ubico: Guatemala, 1931–1944*. Athens: Ohio University Press, 1979.

McCreery, David J. *Development and the State in Reforma Guatemala, 1871–1885*. Athens: Ohio University Press, 1983.

Wagner, Regina. *History of Coffee in Guatemala* (tr. Eric Stull). Bogotá: Villegas, 2001.

Williams, Robert G. *States and Social Evolution: Coffee and the Rise of National Governments in Central America*. Chapel Hill: University of North Carolina Press, 1994.

Chapter 7: The Ten Years of Spring

Adams, Richard N. *Crucifixion by Power: Essays on Guatemalan National Social Structure, 1944–1966*. Austin: University of Texas Press, 1970.

Gleijeses, Piero. *Shattered Hope: The Guatemalan Revolution and the United States, 1944–1954*. Princeton, New Jersey: Princeton University Press, 1991.

Handy, Jim. *Revolution in the Countryside: Rural Conflict & Agrarian Reform in Guatemala, 1944–1954*. Chapel Hill: University of North Carolina Press, 1994.

Immerman, Richard H. *The CIA in Guatemala: The Foreign Policy of Intervention.* Austin: University of Texas Press, 1982.

Schlesinger, Stephen, and Stephen Kinzer. *Bitter Fruit: The Story of the American Coup in Guatemala,* expanded ed. Cambridge, Massachusetts: Harvard University Press, 1999.

Woodward, Jr., Ralph Lee, ed. *Central America: Historical Perspectives on the Contemporary Crises.* Westport, Connecticut: Greenwood Press, 1988.

CHAPTER 8: THE THIRTY YEARS WAR

Black, George, Milton Jamail, and Norma Stoltz Chinchilla. *Garrison Guatemala*. New York: Monthly Review Press, 1984:

Carmack, Robert M., ed. *Harvest of Violence: The Maya Indians and the Guatemalan Crisis*. Norman: University of Oklahoma Press, 1988.

Dosal, Paul J. *Power in Transition: The Rise of Guatemala's Industrial Oligarchy, 1871–1994*. Westport, Connecticut: Praeger, 1995.

Dunkerley, James. *Power in the Isthmus: A Political History of Modern Central America*. London: Verso, 1988.

Ebel, Roland H. *Misunderstood Caudillo: Miguel Ydígoras Fuentes and the Failure of Democracy in Guatemala*. Lanham, Maryland: University Press of America, 1998.

Erlick, June Carolyn. *Disappeared: A Journalist Silenced: The Irma Flaquer Story.* Emeryville, California: Seal Press, 2004.

Garrard-Burnett, Virginia. *Protestantism in Guatemala: Living in the New Jerusalem.* Austin: University of Texas Press, 1998.

Grandin, Greg. *The Last Colonial Massacre: Latin America in the Cold War*. Chicago: University of Chicago Press, 2004.

Levenson-Estrada, Deborah. *Trade Unionists against Terror: Guatemala City: 1954–1985*. Chapel Hill: University of North Carolina Press, 1994.

May, Rachel. *Terror in the Countryside: Campesino Responses to Political Violence in Guatemala, 1954–1985*. Athens: Ohio University Press, 2001.

Menchú, Rigoberta. *I, Rigoberta Menchú: An Indian Woman in Guatemala*, edited by Elisabeth Burgos-Debray (tr. Ann Wright). London: Verso, 1984.

Pereira, Victor. *Unfinished Conquest: The Guatemalan Tragedy*. Berkeley: University of California Press, 1993.

Streeter, Stephen M. *Managing the Counterrevolution: The United States and Guatemala, 1954–1961*. Athens: Ohio University Center for International Studies, 2000.

Wilkinson, Daniel. *Silence on the Mountain: Stories of Terror, Betrayal, and Forgetting in Guatemala*. Durham, North Carolina: Duke University Press, 2004.

Ydígoras Fuentes, Miguel. *My War with Communism*. Englewood Cliffs, New Jersey: Prentice-Hall, 1963.

Chapter 9: Contemporary Guatemala

Chase-Dunn, Christopher, Susanne Jonas, and Nelson Amaro. *Globalization on the Ground: Postbellum Guatemalan Democracy and Development.* Oxford: Rowman & Littlefield, 2001.

McCleary, Rachel. *Dictating Democracy: Guatemala and the End of Violent Revolution*. Gainesville: University Press of Florida, 1999.

Moser, Caroline, and Cathy McIlwaine. *Encounters with Violence in Latin America: Perceptions from Colombia and Guatemala*. New York: Routledge, 2004.

National Human Development Advisory Committee. *Belize: 2002 Poverty Assessment Report*. Belize: Government of Belize, 2004.

World Bank. *Poverty in Guatemala (A World Bank Country Study)*. Washington: World Bank, 2004.

Index